Cancellation of Removal for Lawful Permanent Resident

ATTORNEY BRIAN D. LERNER

Law Offices of Brian D. Lerner, A Professional Corporation

Hello there

CONTACT ME

Phone :
(562) 495-0554

Email :
blerner@californiaimmigration.us

Website:
www.californiaimmigration.us

Welcome to the Law Offices of Brian D. Lerner, APC. In short, we are an Immigration & Nationality Law firm with clients all over the U.S. and in many different countries. As a result, our practice focuses in the areas of Deportation/Removal Representation, Citizenship, Green Cards, Waivers, Appeals. Therefore, we are some of the best Immigration Lawyers in Los Angeles.

Get the best Immigration Attorney to help you. Our immigration lawyer Los Angeles has clients all over the U.S., 30 years of experience and is a certified expert in Immigration Law.

Get an initial free consultation. Firstly, we will determine what are the immigration issues, how we can help you and what is necessary to keep your family together. Secondly, we will see how you can stay in the U.S. or to get to the U.S. Finally, we have over 30 years of experience.

- Attorney Brian D. Lerner

Location

ADDRESS

Long Beach Office Building 3233
E. Broadway, Long Beach, CA
90803

Cancellation of Removal for Lawful Permanent Resident

Print ISBN: 978-1-948774-61-1
Ebook ISBN: 978-1-948774-62-8

Introduction

There are a multitude of different immigration petitions and applications. They are complex and full of r e q u i r e m e n t s . Obviously it would be best to hire and immigration attorney to best prepare the petitions and application. However, this can certainly cost thousands of dollars.

The next best option is to get a sample of the petition written by an experienced immigration attorney. The samples cost a fraction what would be charged by an i m m i g r a t i o n attorney. However, while the reader has to alter, amend and change the parts of the sample petition to reflect their actual situation, it is a fantastic road-map for them to use. If the reader has purchased the entire petition or application, they will have real live samples of cover letters, forms, declarations, affidavits and the necessary exhibits to use. The samples come from real cases and the names of those clients have been redacted to protect the privacy of that person or corporation.

These are petitions and applications that have been drafted by an experienced immigration attorney with over 25 years of experience. Get the benefits of that experience without the costs.

ABOUT THE LAW OFFICES OF BRIAN D. LERNER

Brian D. Lerner has been a licensed attorney since 1992 and started the Law Offices of Brian D. Lerner, APC. The law practice consists of Immigration and Nationality Law and everything involved with and regarding immigration which includes citizenship, investment visas, family and employment visas, removal and deportation hearings, appeals, waivers, adjustment, consulate processing and all types of immigration and citizenship matters. Thousands of families have been reunited and/or permitted to stay in the U.S. and/or return to the U.S. because of the successful work of Immigration Attorney Brian D. Lerner.

This law office handles all types of immigration cases including family based and employment based. Immigration issues range from immigration court proceedings to trying to fix what paralegals may have done that was neither correct nor proper. Foreign nationals must have experienced lawyers admitted to practice law.

The Law Offices of Brian D. Lerner, APC handles cases arising from business visas, work permits, Green Cards, non-immigrant visas, deportation, citizenship, appeals and all areas of immigration. The Law Offices of Brian D. Lerner, APC does EB-5 Investor Visas, H-1B Specialty Occupation, L-1 Intracompany Transferee, E-2 Treaty Investor, E-1 Treaty Trader, O-1 Extraordinary Ability among others. Regarding immigrant visas for the Green Card, the firm does PERM and advanced degree PERM, Family Petitions, and Extraordinary Alien Petitions. In addition to affirmative petitions, the Law Firm represents people in deportation and removal hearings, including political asylum, withholding of removal, and convention against torture cases.

Brian D. Lerner has been certified as an expert in Immigration & Nationality Law by the California State Bar, Board of Legal Specialization since 2000 and has been recertified three times. He now passes on his decades of experience by allowing the Reader, Law Schools, Professors and other Immigration Attorneys to purchase sample petitions on every facet of Immigration Law.

ABOUT A LEGAL PERMANENT RESIDENT CANCELLATION (42A)

A Legal Permanent Resident may have his removal cancelled before a hearing before an Immigration Judge. In order for this to happen, the Legal Permanent Resident has had this status for 5 years, he has had at least 7 years continuous residence in the United States after having been lawfully admitted in any status, and has not been convinced of an aggravated felony. Also has the Form EOIR-42A attached.

TABLE OF CONTENTS

ATTORNEY COVER LETTER

Brian D. Lerner (Bar No. 158536)
Christopher A. Reed (Bar No. 235438)
Law Offices of Brian D. Lerner, APC
3233 E. Broadway
Long Beach, California 90803
Telephone: (562) 495-0554
Facsimile: (562) 608-8672

Attorneys for Respondent

UNITED STATES DEPARTMENT OF JUSTICE

EXECUTIVE OFFICE FOR IMMIGRATION REVIEW

IMMIGRATION COURT

LOS ANGELES, CALIFORNIA

In the Matter of:

███████████████████   File No: ████████████

Respondent,

In Removal Proceedings.

Immigration Judge: Monica Little   Master September 24, 2014 at 8:00 a.m.

**APPLICATION FOR CANCELLATION OF REMOVAL FOR CERTAIN PERMANENT
RESIDENTS AND SUPPORTING DOCUMENTS**

1

TABLE OF CONTENTS

Form:	Description:	
EOIR-42A	Application for Cancellation of Removal for Certain Permanent Residents and Receipt Notice	

FORM EOIR – 42A

U.S. Department of Justice
Executive Office for Immigration Review

OMB#1125-0001

Application for Cancellation of Removal for Certain Permanent Residents

**PLEASE READ ADVICE AND INSTRUCTIONS
BEFORE FILLING IN FORM**

PLEASE TYPE OR PRINT

Fee Stamp (Official Use Only)

PART 1 - INFORMATION ABOUT YOURSELF

1) My present true name is: *(Last, First, Middle)* ▮▮▮▮▮▮	2) Alien Registration (or "A") Number(s): ▮▮▮▮
3) My name given at birth was: *(Last, First, Middle)* ▮▮▮▮▮▮	4) Birth Place: *(City and Country)* Mauban Phillipines

5) Date of Birth: *(Month, Day, Year)* 01/26/1979	6) Gender: ☐ Male ☒ Female	7) Height: 5'2"	8) Hair Color: Black	9) Eye Color: Brown

10) Current Nationality and Citizenship: Philippines Philippines	11) Social Security Number: ▮▮▮▮	12) Home Phone Number: ▮▮▮▮	13) Work Phone Number: ▮▮▮▮

14) I currently reside at: ▮	15) I have been known by these additional name(s):
Apt. number and/or in care of ▮▮▮▮	N/A
Number and Street Los Angeles CA 90026	
City or Town *State* *Zip Code*	

16) I have resided in the following locations in the United States: (List PRESENT ADDRESS FIRST, and work back in time for at least 7 years.)

Street and Number - Apt. or Room # - City or Town - State - Zip Code	Resided From: *(Month, Day, Year)*	Resided To: *(Month, Day, Year)*
▮▮▮▮▮▮	10/2006	PRESENT

PART 2 - INFORMATION ABOUT THIS APPLICATION

17) I, the undersigned, hereby request that my removal be cancelled under the provisions of section 240A(a) of the Immigration and Nationality Act (INA). I believe that I am eligible for this relief because I have been a lawful permanent resident alien for 5 or more years, have 7 years of continuous residence in the United States, and have not been convicted of an aggravated felony. I was admitted as or adjusted to the status of an alien lawfully admitted for permanent residence on <u>02/11/1989</u>

(Date)

at <u>Los Angeles, CA</u>

(Place)

3847

PART 3 - INFORMATION ABOUT YOUR PRESENCE IN THE UNITED STATES

18) My first arrival into the United States was under the name of: *(Last, First, Middle)*

▮▮▮▮▮▮▮▮▮▮

19) My first arrival to the United States was on: *(Month, Day, Year)*

02/11/1989

20) Place or port of first arrival: *(Place or Port, City, and State)*

LAX, Los Angeles, CA

21) I: ☒ was inspected and admitted.

☒ I entered using my Lawful Permanent Resident card which is valid until _____ *(Month, Day, Year)*

☐ I entered using a _____ *(Specify Type of Visa)* visa which is valid until _____ *(Month, Day, Year)*

☐ was not inspected and admitted.

☐ I entered without documents. Explain: _____

☐ I entered without inspection. Explain: _____

☐ Other. Explain: _____

22) I applied on _____ *(Month, Day, Year)* for additional time to stay and it was ☐ granted on _____ *(Month, Day, Year)*

and valid until _____ *(Month, Day, Year)*, or ☐ denied on _____ *(Month, Day, Year)*

23) Since the date of my first entry, I departed from and returned to the United States at the following places and on the following dates:

(Please list all departures regardless of how briefly you were absent from the United States.)

If you have never departed from the United States since your original date of entry, please mark an X in this box: ☐

	Port of Departure *(Place or Port, City and State)*	Departure Date *(Month, Day, Year)*	Purpose of Travel	Destination
1	MIA	06/~~2013~~ 2012	Vacation	Bahamas
	Port of Return *(Place or Port, City and State)*	Return Date *(Month, Day, Year)*	Manner of Return	Inspected and Admitted?
	MIA	06/~~2013~~ 2012	Air	☒ Yes ☐ No
2	Port of Departure *(Place or Port, City and State)*	Departure Date *(Month, Day, Year)*	Purpose of Travel	Destination
	LAX	1997	Vacation	Philippines
	Port of Return *(Place or Port, City and State)*	Return Date *(Month, Day, Year)*	Manner of Return	Inspected and Admitted?
	LAX	1997	Air	☒ Yes ☐ No

24) Have you ever departed the United States:

a) under an order of deportation, exclusion, or removal? .... ☐ Yes ☒ No

b) pursuant to a grant of voluntary departure? .... ☐ Yes ☒ No

PART 4 - INFORMATION ABOUT YOUR MARITAL STATUS AND SPOUSE *(Continued on page 3)*

25) I am not married: ☒
I am married: ☐

26) If married, the name of my spouse is: *(Last, First, Middle)*

27) My spouse's name before marriage was:

28) The marriage took place in: *(City and Country)*

29) Date of marriage: *(Month, Day, Year)*

30) My spouse currently resides at:

Apt. number and/or in care of

Number and Street

City or Town   State/Country   Zip Code

31) Place and date of birth of my spouse: *(City & Country; Month, Day, Year)*

32) My spouse is a citizen of: *(Country)*

33) If your spouse is other than a native born United States citizen, answer the following:

He/she arrived in the United States at: *(Place or Port, City and State)* _____

He/she arrived in the United States on: *(Month, Day, Year)* _____

His/her alien registration number(s) is: A# _____

He/she was naturalized on: *(Month, Day, Year)* _____ at _____ *(City and State)*

34) My spouse ☐ - is ☐ - is not employed. If employed, please give salary and the name and address of the place(s) of employment.

Full Name and Address of Employer	Earnings Per Week *(Approximate)*
	$
	$
	$

PART 4 - INFORMATION ABOUT YOUR MARITAL STATUS AND SPOUSE (Continued)

35) I ☐ - have ☒ - have not been previously married: (If previously married, list the name of each prior spouse, the dates on which each marriage began and ended, the place where the marriage terminated, and describe how each marriage ended.)

Name of prior spouse: (Last, First, Middle)	Date marriage began: Date marriage ended:	Place marriage ended: (City and Country)	Description or manner of how marriage was terminated or ended:

Name of prior spouse: (Last, First, Middle)	Date marriage began: Date marriage ended:	Place marriage ended: (City and Country)	Description or manner of how marriage was terminated or ended:

36) Have you been ordered by any court, or are otherwise under any legal obligation, to provide child support and/or spousal maintenance as a result of a separation and/or divorce? ☐ - Yes ☒ - No

PART 5 - INFORMATION ABOUT YOUR EMPLOYMENT AND FINANCIAL STATUS

37) Since my arrival into the United States, I have been employed by the following named persons or firms: (Please begin with present employment and work back in time. Any periods of unemployment or school attendance should be specified. Attach a separate sheet for additional entries if necessary.)

Full Name and Address of Employer	Earnings Per Week (Approximate)	Type of Work Performed	Employed From: (Month, Day, Year)	Employed To: (Month, Day, Year)
████████████	$ 500	Caregiver	2011	PRESENT 2014
████████████	$ 250	Hostess/Dealer	2000	2002
████████████	$ 150	Cashier	1993	1993

38) If self-employed, describe the nature of the business, the name of the business, its address, and net income derived therefrom:

39) My assets (and if married, my spouse's assets) in the United States and other countries, not including clothing and household necessities, are:

Self		Jointly Owned With Spouse	
Cash, Stocks, and Bonds................. $	0	Cash, Stocks, and Bonds............................ $	
Real Estate.................................. $	0	Real Estate... $	
Auto (dollar value minus amount owed) ..... $	0	Auto (dollar value minus amount owed)........ $	
Other (describe on line below)................... $	0	Other (describe on line below)...................... $	
0 TOTAL $		TOTAL $	

40) I ☒ - have ☐ - have not received public or private relief or assistance (e.g. Welfare, Unemployment Benefits, Medicaid, TANF, AFDC, etc.). If you have, please give full details including the type of relief or assistance received, date for which relief or assistance was received, place, and total amount received during this time:

2010-2012 - Food Stamps and Cash Aid

41) Please list each of the years in which you have filed an income tax return with the Internal Revenue Service: _____

2000-2002

42) I have _____ **0** _____ (Number of) children. Please list information for each child below, include assets and earnings information for children over the age of 16 who have separate incomes:

Name of Child: (Last, First, Middle) Child's Alien Registration Number:	Citizen of What Country: Birth Date: (Month, Day, Year)	Now Residing At: (City and Country) Birth Date: (City and Country)	Immigration Status of Child
A#:			
Estimated Total of Assets: $ _____	Estimated Average Weekly Earnings: $ _____		
A#:			
Estimated Total of Assets: $ _____	Estimated Average Weekly Earnings: $ _____		
A#:			
Estimated Total of Assets: $ _____	Estimated Average Weekly Earnings: $ _____		

43) If your application is denied, would your spouse and all of your children accompany you to your:

If you answered "No" to any of the responses, please explain: _____

Country of Birth - ☐ Yes ☐ No

N/A

Country of Nationality - ☐ Yes ☐ No

Country of Last Residence - ☐ Yes ☐ No

44) Members of my family, including my spouse and/or child(ren) ☐ - have ☒ - have not received public or private relief or assistance (e.g., Welfare, Unemployment Benefits, Medicaid, TANF, AFDC, etc.). If any member of your immediate family has received such relief or assistance, please give full details including identity of person(s) receiving relief or assistance, dates for which relief or assistance was received, place, and total amount received during this time:

45) Please give the requested information about your parents, brothers, sisters, aunts, uncles, and grandparents, living or deceased. As to residence, show street address, city, and state, if in the United States; otherwise show only country:

Name: (Last, First, Middle) Alien Registration Number:	Citizen of What Country: Birth Date: (Month, Day, Year)	Relationship to Me: Birth Date: (City and Country)		Immigration Status of Listed Relative
████████ A#: ████████	Philippines 06/28/1952	Father Mauban	Philippines	LPR
Complete Address of Current Residence, if Living: ██████████				
████████ A#: N/A	USA 03/12/1956	Mother Mauban	Philippines	USA
Complete Address of Current Residence, if Living: ██████████				

PART 7 - MISCELLANEOUS INFORMATION *(Continued on page 6)*

46) I ☐ - have ☒ - have not entered the United States as a crewman after June 30, 1964.

47) I ☐ - have ☒ - have not been admitted as, or after arrival in the United States acquired the status of, an exchange alien.

48) I ☒ - have ☐ - have not submitted address reports as required by section 265 of the Immigration and Nationality Act.

49) I ☒ - have ☐ - have never (either in the United States or in any foreign country) been arrested, summoned into court as a defendant, convicted, fined, imprisoned, placed on probation, or forfeited collateral for an act involving a felony, misdemeanor, or breach of any public law or ordinance (including, but not limited to, traffic violations or driving incidents involving alcohol). *(If answer is in the affirmative, please give a brief description of each offense including the name and location of the offense, date of conviction, any penalty imposed, any sentence imposed, and the time actually served.)*

07/24/2007 - misdemeanor credit/debit card fraud in violation of section 484E(d) of the California Penal Code. 36 months probation, 3 days jail.

12/29/2008 - felony possession of a controlled substance in violation of section 11337(a) of the California Health and Safety Code. 24 months probation, 2 days jail.

12/29/2008 - felony possession of a controlled substance in violation of section 11337(a) of the California Health and Safety Code. 24 months probation, 1 day jail.

50) Have you ever served in the Armed Forces of the United States? ☐ - Yes ☒ - No. If "Yes" please state branch *(Army, Navy, etc.)* and service number: _____

Place of entry on duty: *(City and State)* _____

Date of entry on duty: *(Month, Day, Year)* _____ Date of discharge: *(Month, Day, Year)* _____

Type of discharge: *(Honorable, Dishonorable, etc.)* _____

I served in active duty status from: *(Month, Day, Year)* _____ to *(Month, Day, Year)* _____

51) Have you ever left the United States or the jurisdiction of the district where you registered for the draft to avoid being drafted into the military or naval forces of the United States? ☐ Yes ☒ No

52) Have you ever deserted from the military or naval forces of the United States while the United States was at war? ☐ Yes ☒ No

53) If male, did you register under the Military Selective Service Act or any applicable previous Selective Service (Draft) Laws? ☐ Yes ☐ No
If "Yes," please give date, Selective Service number, local draft board number, and your last draft classification: _____

54) Were you ever exempted from service because of conscientious objection, alienage, or any other reason? ☐ Yes ☒ No

55) Please list your present or past membership in or affiliation with every political organization, association, fund, foundation, party, club, society, or similar group in the United States or any other place since your 16th birthday. Include any foreign military service in this part. If none, write "None." Include the name of the organization, location, nature of the organization, and the dates of membership.

Name of Organization	Location of Organization	Nature of Organization	Member From: *(Month, Day, Year)*	Member To: *(Month, Day, Year)*

Form EOIR-42A
Revised October 2013

56) Have you ever:

☐ Yes ☒ No been ordered deported, excluded, or removed?

☐ Yes ☒ No overstayed a grant of voluntary departure from an Immigration Judge or the Department of Homeland Security (DHS), formerly the Immigration and Naturalization Service (INS)?

☐ Yes ☒ No failed to appear for deportation or removal?

57) Have you ever been:

☐ Yes ☒ No a habitual drunkard?

☐ Yes ☒ No one whose income is derived principally from illegal gambling?

☐ Yes ☒ No one who has given false testimony for the purpose of obtaining immigration benefits?

☐ Yes ☒ No one who has engaged in prostitution or unlawful commercialized vice?

☐ Yes ☒ No involved in a serious criminal offense and asserted immunity from prosecution?

☐ Yes ☒ No a polygamist?

☐ Yes ☒ No one who brought in or attempted to bring in another to the United States illegally?

☐ Yes ☒ No a trafficker of a controlled substance, or a knowing assister, abettor, conspirator, or colluder with others in any such controlled substance offense (not including a single offense of simple possession of 30 grams or less of marijuana)?

☐ Yes ☒ No inadmissible or deportable on security-related grounds under sections 212(a)(3) or 237(a)(4) of the INA?

☐ Yes ☒ No one who has ordered, incited, assisted, or otherwise participated in the persecution of an individual on account of his or her race, religion, nationality, membership in a particular social group, or political opinion?

☐ Yes ☒ No a person previously granted relief under sections 212(c) or 244(a) of the INA or whose removal has previously been cancelled under section 240A of the INA?

If you answered "Yes" to any of the above questions, explain:

58) The following certificates or other supporting documents are attached hereto as a part of this application: *(Refer to the Instructions for*

See Attached

Please continue answers on a separate sheet as needed.

(6)

PART 8 - SIGNATURE OF PERSON PREPARING FORM, IF OTHER THAN APPLICANT

(Read the following information and sign below)

I declare that I have prepared this application at the request of the person named in Part 1, that the responses provided are based on all information of which I have knowledge, or which was provided to me by the applicant, and that the completed application was read to the applicant in a language the applicant speaks fluently for verification before he or she signed the application in my presence. I am aware that the knowing placement of false information on the Form EOIR-42A may subject me to civil penalties under 8 U.S.C. 1324c.

Signature of Preparer:	Print Name: Christopher A. Reed	Date: 08/28/2014
Daytime Telephone #: (562) 495-0554	Address of Preparer: *(Number and Street, City, State, Zip Code)* Law Offices of Brian D. Lerner, APC 3233 E. Broadway Long Beach, CA 90803	

PART 9 - SIGNATURE

APPLICATION NOT TO BE SIGNED BELOW UNTIL APPLICANT APPEARS BEFORE AN IMMIGRATION JUDGE

I swear or affirm that I know the contents of this application that I am signing, including the attached documents and supplements, and that they are all true to the best of my knowledge, taking into account the correction(s) numbered _____ to _____, if any, that were made by me or at my request.

_____
(Signature of Applicant or Parent or Guardian)

Subscribed and sworn to before me by the above-named applicant at _____

_____
Immigration Judge

_____
Date: (Month, Day, Year)

PART 10 - PROOF OF SERVICE

I hereby certify that a copy of the foregoing Form EOIR-42A was: ☐ - delivered in person   ☐ - mailed first class, postage prepaid

on _____ to the Assistant Chief Counsel for the DHS (U.S. Immigration and Customs Enforcement-ICE)
(Month, Day, Year)

at _____
(Number and Street, City, State, Zip Code)

_____
Signature of Applicant (or Attorney or Representative)

Please continue answers on a separate sheet as needed.

(7)

Form EOIR-42A
Revised October 2013

9

Addendum

█████████████████████████ ı, Form: EOIR-42A, A# 042-049-242 , 08/28/2014 (Page 1)

Part 3. 23) Additional Departure/Arrival History:

Port of Departure: LAX
Departure Date: 1994
Purpose of Travel: Vacation
Destination: Philippines
Port of Return: LAX
Return Date: 1994
Inspected and Admitted?: Yes

Part 6. 45) Additional Relatives:

████████████████████████████

Citizenship: Philippines
DOB: 09/25/1975
Place and Country of Birth: Mauban, Philippines
████████████████████████████

Immigration Status: LPR

████████████████████████████

Citizenship: USA
DOB: 10/29/1981
Place and Country of Birth: Mauban, Philippines
████████████████████████████

Immigration Status: USC

Department of Homeland Security
U.S. Citizenship and Immigration Service.

Form I-797C, Notice of Action

THIS NOTICE DOES NOT GRANT ANY IMMIGRATION STATUS OR BENEFIT.

RECEIPT NUMBER		CASE TYPE	EOIR 42A Application for Cancellation of Removal for Certain Permanent Residents
SRC-14-237-50478			
RECEIVED DATE	PRIORITY DATE	APPLICANT	
SEPTEMBER 03, 2014			
NOTICE DATE	PAGE	PRINCIPAL ALIEN	
SEPTEMBER 5, 2014	1 of 1		

CHRISTOPHER REED
LAW OFFICES OF BRIAN D LERNER
3233 E BROADWAY
LONG BEACH CA 90803

Notice Type: Receipt Notice
Amount received: $100.00

This notice acknowledges the above receipt of your designated application and fee
as part of the requirements before the immigration judge can grant relief in your case.

The above application has been received and accepted as an I-485 receipt at the Texas Service Center.
The actual case you submitted is listed in the block marked 'CASE TYPE'

Please notify us immediately if any of the above information is incorrect.

A fingerprint appointment will be scheduled and you will be notified at a later date.

Always remember to call customer service if you move while your case is pending.

You will be notified separately about any other cases you have filed.

CITIZENSHIP & IMMIGRATION SERVICE
TEXAS SERVICE CENTER
P O BOX 851488 - DEPT A
MESQUITE, TX 751851488
Customer Service Telephone: (800) 375-5283

Please see the back of this notice for important information.

TABS

TAB A
Respondent's Certificate of Live Birth

MUNICIPAL FORM No. 102 — (Revised Dec. 1, 1958)

(TO BE ACCOMPLISHED IN DUPLICATE)

REPUBLIC OF THE PHILIPPINES

CERTIFICATE OF LIVE BIRTH
(FILL OUT COMPLETELY, ACCURATELY, LEGIBLY IN INK OR TYPEWRITER)

Register Number:

Province: **Quezon**

City or Municipality: **Mauban**

(a) Civil Registrar-General No.

(b) Local Civil Registrar No.

1. PLACE OF BIRTH		**2.** USUAL RESIDENCE OF MOTHER (Where does mother live?)
a. PROVINCE **Quezon**		a. PROVINCE **Quezon**
b. CITY OR MUNICIPALITY **Mauban**		b. CITY OR MUNICIPALITY **Mauban**
c. NAME OF HOSPITAL OR INSTITUTION (If not in hospital, give street address):		c. NUMBER AND STREET **31 Liwana St.**
d. IS PLACE OF BIRTH INSIDE CITY LIMITS?		d. IS RESIDENCE INSIDE CITY LIMITS? e. IS RESIDENCE ON A FARM?
YES ☐ NO ☐		YES ☐ NO ☐ YES ☐ NO ☐

CHILD

3. NAME (Type or print)	First	Middle ██████	Last

4. SEX ██	5a. THIS BIRTH SINGLE ☒ TWIN ☐ TRIPLET ☐	5b. IF TWIN OR TRIPLET, WAS CHILD 1ST ☐ 2ND ☐ 3RD ☐	6. DATE OF BIRTH Month **Jan.** Day **26** Year **1979**

FATHER

7. NAME	First **Horacio**	Middle **Villamayor**	Last **Unilayao**	RELIGION **Catholic**	8. NATIONALITY **Filipino**	8a. RACE **Brown**

9. AGE (At time of this birth) Years **27**	10. BIRTHPLACE **Mauban, Quezon**	11a. USUAL OCCUPATION **Laborer**	11b. KIND OF BUSINESS OR INDUSTRY

MOTHER

12. MAIDEN NAME	First **Solita**	Middle **de los Santos**	Last **Estava**	RELIGION **Catholic**	13. NATIONALITY **Filipino**	13b. RACE **Brown**

14. AGE (At time of this birth) Years **23**	15. BIRTHPLACE **Mauban, Quezon**	16. PREVIOUS DELIVERIES TO MOTHER (Do not include this birth):		
		a. How many children are now living? **1**	b. How many other children were born alive but are now dead? **0**	c. How many fetal deaths (fetuses born dead any time after conception)? **0**

17a. INFORMANT'S SIGNATURE		
b. NAME IN PRINT: ██████		
c. ADDRESS		

18. MOTHER'S MAILING ADDRESS: (Number, Street, City or Municipality, Province) **31 Liwana St., Mauban, Quezon**

ATTENDANT AT BIRTH

19.	d. DATE SIGNED BY ATTENDANT AT BIRTH:
I HEREBY CERTIFY that I attended the birth of this child who was born alive at **4:00** o'clock **A.** M. on the date above indicated.	e. TITLE OF ATTENDANT AT BIRTH: ☐ M. D. ☐ MIDWIFE ☐ NURSE ☒ OTHERS (Specify) **Hilot**
a. SIGNATURE:	
b. NAME IN PRINT: **JULITA NAVA**	
c. ADDRESS: **Mauban, Quezon**	21. a. GIVEN NAME ADDED FROM SUPPLEMENTAL REPORT:
20. RECEIVED IN THE OFFICE ... BY:	
a. SIGNATURE:	b. DATE WHEN GIVEN NAME WAS SUPPLIED:
b. NAME IN PRINT: **PABLO A. de SILVA**	
c. TITLE OR POSITION: **Local Civil Registrar**	
d. DATE:	

22a. LENGTH OF PREGNANCY COMPLETED WEEKS:	22b. WEIGHT AT BIRTH Lbs. Oz.	23. LEGITIMATE ☒ YES ☐ NO

24. DATE AND PLACE OF MARRIAGE OF PARENTS (For legitimate birth) **July 25 1975** (Month) (Date) (Year) City or Municipality **Lucena** Province **City**	25. THIS CERTIFICATE IS PREPARED BY: SIGNATURE: NAME IN PRINT: **LEONILA C. VELASCO** TITLE OR POSITION: **Civ. Reg. & Statistic.** DATE: **Feb. Clerk 2-6-79**

18-239.   (SPACE FOR MEDICAL AND HEALTH ITEMS FOR SPECIAL PURPOSES)

Republic of the Philippines
Municipality of Mauban
Quezon
OFFICE OF THE LOCAL CIVIL REGISTRAR

TO WHOM IT MAY CONCERN:

This is to certify that according to the records on file in this office the following is the records of birth of one; ██████████████████, to wit:

Name of Child - - - - - - - -
Date of Birth - - - - - - -
Name of Father - - - - - - -
Nationality - - - - - - - -
Name of Mother - - - - - -
Nationality - - - - - - - -
Legitimate - - - - - - - -
Nationality - - - - - - - -
Register of Birth - - - - - -
Page - - - - - - - - - - -
Line No. - - - - - - - - -
Book No. - - - - - - - - - XV- Chronological Order

Issued this __14th__ day of __January__, 19__83__ at Mauban, Quezon.

Paid Under O.R. No. 9843274
Date **January 14,** , 19 __83__
Amount ₱ 5.00

rolly/1/8/83

PABLO A. de SILVA
Local Civil Registrar

BY:
JESUS C. FOLLANTE
Asst. Local Civil Registrar
& Asst. Municipal Treasurer

2

TAB B
Respondent's Certificate of Baptism

Certificate of Baptism

DIOCESE OF LUCENA
Parish of St. Bonaventure
Mauban, Quezon

THIS IS TO CERTIFY

That ████████████████

Child of ████████████████

and ....

born in MAUBAN, QUEZON .... on the

26th day of JANUARY ...., 19 79.. was solemnly BAPTIZED

on the 19th day of AUGUST ...., 1979..

ACCORDING TO THE RITE OF THE
ROMAN CATHOLIC CHURCH

by the Rev. FR. BENJAMIN L. RODA JR. ....

the Sponsors being ████████████ ....

and ████████████ ....

the Baptismal Register No. 42 Page 40 Line 8

of this Church.

Dated October 23...., 19 84.

Purpose: for reference

REV. FR. DOMINGO B. EDORA
PARISH PRIEST
by: _____
Parish sec

16

4

TAB C
Respondent's I-94, Social Security Card and Passport

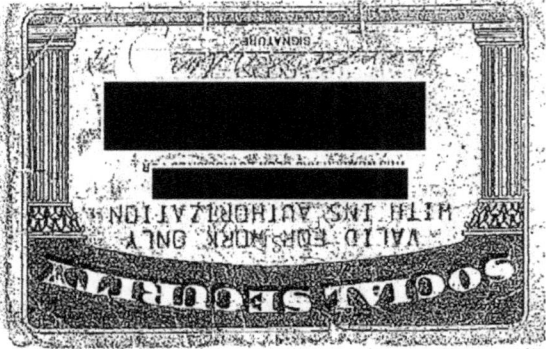

on enter...nt serves as
...porary I-551 evidencing
...manent residency.
...e Date 08 AUG 2012   C
...ficer AX0270   B
...LOYMENT AUTHORIZED   P
...ntil 09 AUG 2013

C27023

. Family Name

. First (Given) Name   3. Birth Date (Day/Mo/Yr)
                                          2 6 10 1 1 7 9

4. Country of Citizenship   5. Sex (Male or Female)
PHILIPPINES   FEMALE

6. Passport Number   7. Airline and Flight Number

8. Country Where You Live   9. City Where You Boarded
USA

10. City Where Visa Was Issued   11. Date Issued (Day/Mo/Yr)

12. Address While in the United States (Number and Street)

13. City and State
LOS ANGELES, CA 90026

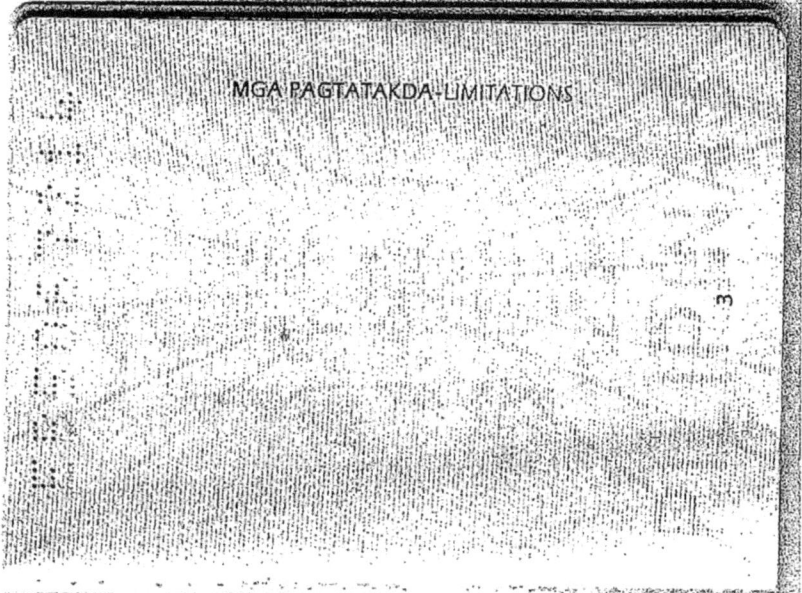

REPUBLIKA NG PILIPINAS / REPUBLIC OF THE PHILIPPINES

PASAPORTE
PASSPORT   P   PHL   EB6067214

26 Jan 79   FILIPINO

F   MAUBAN QUEZON

02 Apr 12   PCG LOS ANGELES

01 Apr 17

TAB D
Respondent's School Records

Consideration of Deferred Action for Childhood Arrivals

Record of Enrollment

Date	MARCH 25, 2014
Current **Last** Name	
Current **First** Name	
Current **Middle** Initial	
Student **Last** Name (at time of attendance)	
Student **First** Name (at time of attendance)	
Student **Middle** Initial (at time of attendance)	
Student DOB	
Address, City, State, Zip Code (of record)	
Date of District Enrollment	9/7/1994
Years of Enrollment	4

Status of District Enrollment

CURRENT   Current Student ◯ Yes   ◉ No

Current School	
School Address	
Current Grade Level	
Name of Program (i.e. ESL, GED, Job Training)	

GRADUATE   Graduate ◯ Yes   ◉ No

Graduation Month/Year	
High School Attended	
School Address	
Name of Program (i.e. ESL, GED, Job Training)	

GED   GED Completion ◯ Yes   ◉ No

School Attended	
School Address	
GED Completion Month/Year	

Ambra D. Dorsey, J.D.
Custodian of Records

MANDATORY PERMANENT RECORD
(CUMULATIVE FOLDER) ELEMENTARY

3330/81 | 01-26-79 FB
GRADE: 04

SCHOOL 15
STUDENT IDENTIFIED AS IFP

Legal Name

Place of Birth: Phillipines
City: State: FB
Date of Birth: 1-26-79

How Verified
Baptismal Record ☐ Affidavit ☐ Sex F ☑ T-Twin ☐ Blank - No

Grades repeated: ☐

Date Entered	School	Home Address	Zip Code	Phone	Trans. to			Date
9/5/89	Del Mar		93704					3/6/92
3-9-92	Pyle		93726					6-92

Grade and Room Number (Use Pencil)
Pre Sch	K	1	2	3				S.P.
					8	2	5	18
								6

TRANSCRIPT REC
Sent to

FATHER
Name (Last) (First) (Middle)
Address: SAME AS STUDENT
(City) (State)
Occupation
(State or Country of Birth) Phillipines (Citizenship) U.S. ☐ Other ☒

MOTHER
Name (Last) Estaya (First) (Middle)
Address: SAME AS STUDENT
(City) (State)
Occupation: Benefit Approver
(State or Country of Birth) Phillipines (Citizenship) U.S. ☒ Other ☐

STEPFATHER STEPMOTHER, GUARDIAN OR FOSTER PARENTS
Name (Last) (First) (Middle)
Address
(City) (State)
Occupation
(State or Country of Birth) (Citizenship) U.S. ☐ Other ☐
Year of Birth

List all other children in the household.
		Year of Birth			Year of Birth
1.	Edmund	75	7.		
2.	Allysa	85	8.		
3.			9.		

ADULT CODE	LANG OF HOME	ETHNIC CODE	SPEC. ED. CODE	HEALTH CODE	GU
1	3	6			

Child Lives With (Use Pencil): parents   Date: 9/5/89

CHDP Complete: _____ Date: _____

(CUMULATIVE FOLDER) ELEMENTARY

SCHOOL: 13
GRADE: 04

STUDENT IDENTIFIED AS LEP
PRIMARY LANGUAGE: TAGALOG
DATE: 09/27/89

Record all grades in permanent black ink
Column a -- Partial grades
Column b -- Final grades

RECORDING REPORT C——————

If achievement and effort marks are given,
record only achievement marks. If effort
only is graded, enter the effort mark.

ACHIEVEMENT
A Superior
B Above Average
C Average
D Fulfillment of minimum req.
F Failure to meet minimum req.
X Not graded this period

MARKS

EFFORT
G Good
S Satisfactory
N Needs to Improve

	Pre School	1st yr.		2nd yr.		3rd yr.		4th yr.		5th yr.		6th yr.		7th yr.		8th yr.		9th yr.
Teacher										Leone		Mum							
Grade										4		5							
School										Bel Mar		Del Mar							
Year In School																			
School Year	19 19	19 19		19 19		19 19		19 19		19 19		19 19		19 19		19 19		19 19
Days Enrolled										E180 A180		E180 A176		E180 A171					
Days Attended										A180		A176		A171					
Reading																			
Mathematics																			
English Oral Language																			
Written Language																			
Handwriting																			
Spelling																			
Social Science																			
Health/Science																			
Physical Education																			
Art																			
Music																			
Instrumental Music Band																			
Orchestra																			
Citizenship																			
Attendance in Summer School																			

PHOTO RECORD

Primary	Intermed
PHOTO	PHOT
PHOTO	

K-Preschool

1

22

10

COURSE TITLE 07	GRADE	EFFORT	ATTITUDE	STUDY HABITS
LANG 7B	A	G	G	G
GEOG 7B	A	G	G	G
EXPLO 7	C	S	S	S
MATH 7B	C	N	S	S
HLTH/L.S. 7B	B	G	G	G
COED P.E.	B	G	G	S
HMRM 7B		S	S	
71	11/06/92			

COURSE TITLE 07	GRADE	EFFORT	ATTITUDE	STUDY HABITS
LANG 7B	A	S	S	S
GEOG 7B	B	N	S	S
EXPLO 7	B	S	S	S
MATH 7B	F	N	S	N
HLTH/L.S. 7B	C	N	S	S
COED P.E.	B	N	N	S
HMRM 7B		G	S	
71	01/29/93			

COURSE TITLE 07	GRADE	EFFORT	ATTITUDE	STUDY HABITS
LANG 7B	B	S	S	S
WRLD HIST 7B	B	S	N	S
HLTH/L.S. 7B	A	G	S	G
PEER COUNS	A	S	G	N
MATH 7B	C	S	S	S
COED P.E.	C	G	G	S
HMRM 7B				
71	04/02/93			

COURSE TITLE 07	GRADE	EFFORT	ATTITUDE	STUDY HABITS
LANG 7B	B	N	S	N
WRLD HIST 7B	C	N	N	N
MATH 7B	D	S	S	S
PEER COUNS	B	S	S	S
HLTH/L.S. 7B	B	N	N	S
COED P.E.	C	S	G	N
HMRM 7B				
71	06/17/93			

9TH GRADE

COURSE TITLE 08	GRADE	EFFORT	ATTITUDE	STUDY HABITS
LANG 8B	B	S	G	S
U.S. HIST 8B	F	N	S	N
SCI 8B	D	S	S	S
COED PE	B	G	G	G
MATH 8B	C	G	G	G
LASER LAB	A	S	S	S
HR8B/7:55AM				
71	11/05/93			

COURSE TITLE 08	GRADE	EFFORT	ATTITUDE	STUDY HABITS
LANG 8B	C	S	S	S
U.S. HIST 8B	C	G	G	S
SCI 8B	D	N	N	S
COED PE	B	G	S	G
MANUFCT RNG 8	E	S	S	G
MATH 8B	D	S	N	N
LASER LAB	A	N	N	S
HR8B/7:55AM				
71	01/28/94			

COURSE TITLE 08	GRADE	EFFORT	ATTITUDE	STUDY HABITS
LANG 8B	F	N	N	N
U.S. HIST 8B	D	S	S	S
SCI 8B	D	S	S	S
COED PE	F	N	N	N
ART	C	N	S	S
MATH 8B	D	S	S	S
HR8B/7:55AM				
71	04/15/94			

8TH GRADE CONSTITUTION TEST FAILED

COURSE TITLE 08	GRADE	EFFORT	ATTITUDE	STUDY HABITS
LANG 8B	F	N	S	N
U.S. HIST 8B	F	N	N	S
SCI 8B	D	N	S	N
COED PE	F	N	S	S
ART	D	S	S	N
MATH 8B	F	N	N	S
HR8B/7:55AM				
71	06/16/94			

EXPLANATION OF TERMS

ACHIEVEMENT:
The quality of accomplishment compared to the expectations for his/her grade level.

EFFORT:
The teacher's assessment of how the student applies himself/herself to the task.

GRADE LEVEL:
Determined by the age designation for the State textbooks and district materials used by the students.

DEFINITION OF MARKS

ACHIEVEMENT
- A Superior
- B Above Average
- C Average
- D Fulfillment of minimum req.
- F Failure to meet minimum req.
- X Not graded this period

EFFORT
- G Good
- S Satisfactory
- N Needs to Improve

COMMENTS

Quarter 1 Conference

Tear off and return to school.

Quarter 2 _[handwritten comments]_

Tear off and return to school.

Quarter 3 Very bright _[handwritten comments]_

Tear off and return to school.

Quarter 4 _[handwritten comments]_

	FIRST PERIOD		SECOND PERIOD		THIRD PERIOD		FOURTH PERIOD	
	ACHIEVEMENT	EFFORT	ACHIEVEMENT	EFFORT	ACHIEVEMENT	EFFORT	ACHIEVEMENT	EFFORT
READING	B	G	A	G	A	G	A	C
MATHEMATICS	A	G	B	C	B	C	B	C
ENGLISH Oral Language*	A	C	B	C	B	C	B	C
Written Language	A	C	B	C	A	G	A	C
HANDWRITING	B	G	B	G	B	G	B	C
SPELLING	G	G	C	G	A	G	A	C
SOCIAL STUDIES	B	G	AB	C	B	C	B	C
HEALTH / SCIENCE**	B	C	B	C	B	C	B	C
PHYSICAL EDUCATION	C	C	C	C	C	C	C	C
ART	C	C	C	C	C	C		C
MUSIC								
INSTRUMENTAL MUSIC Band								
Orchestra								

GRADE LEVEL ACHIEVEMENT

	First Quarter			Second Quarter			Third Quarter			Fourth Quarter		
	Above	On	Below	Above	On	Below	Above	On	Below	Above	On	Below
Rdg												
Math												

CITIZENSHIP	1	2	3	4
Conduct in Class	G	G	S	G
Behavior on Playground	G	G	G	G
Accepts Responsibility	G	G	G	G

ATTENDANCE	1	2	3	4
DAYS ABSENT	0	0	0	0
TIMES TARDY	0	0	0	0
Homework	G	G	G	G

First grade students will be given only effort marks for the 1st report period.

24

12

FRESNO UNIFIED SCHOOL DISTRICT - FRESNO, CALIFORNIA - PERMANENT RECORD FORM   CLASS OF 1999
** HIGH SCHOOL RECORD **

ID#: 333081   BIRTH: 1/26/79   SEX: F | FATHER: HORACIO | MOTHER: SOLITA | GUARDIAN:
GR: 10   BDATE VERIFIED: AFFIDAVIT | CURRENT SCHOOL: RESTART/TCW | SSN: 607-22-1783   BPLACE: FB
LEGAL NAME:

FRESNO, CA 93722

GRADE CODES:				IMMUNIZATIONS --
A-EXCEPTIONAL		CITIZENSHIP:		POLIO 06/27/89 08/11/89 02/28/9
B-ABOVE AVERAGE		S-SATISFACTORY		DTP 06/27/89 08/11/89 02/28/9
C-AVERAGE		P-POOR		MEASLES 06/27/89
D-BELOW AVERAGE		U-UNSATISFACTORY		MUMPS 06/27/89
P-PASS				RUBELLA 06/27/89
E-EXCUSED		COURSE LEVEL:		TB SKIN 08/03/89 RESULT: 15
F-FAILURE		AP-ADVANC PLCMNT		CHEST X 08/03/89 RESULT: N
I-INCOMPLETE		B-BILINGUAL		
N-NO GRADE/NO CREDIT		G-GATE		
W-WITHDRAW/NO PENALTY		H-HONORS		
WF-WITHDRAW/FAIL		I-ENG IMMERSION		
FA-FAIL/ATTENDANCE		P-COLLEGE PREP		
		S-SDAIE		
		SDC-SP DAY CLASS		

GRADUATION REQUIREMENTS

SUBJECT	CREDIT REQUIRED	CREDIT COMPLETED	CREDIT NEEDED
ENGLISH LANGUAGE ARTS	30.0	10.0	20.0
AMERICAN GOVERNMENT	5.0	.0	5.0
U. S. HISTORY	10.0	6.0	4.0
MODERN WORLD HISTORY	10.0	10.0	.0
BIOLOGICAL SCIENCE	10.0	10.0	.0
PHYSICAL SCIENCE	10.0	10.0	.0
MATHEMATICS	20.0	10.0	10.0
PHYSICAL EDUCATION	30.0	15.0	15.0
SOCIOLOGY FOR LIVING	10.0	10.0	.0
FOREIGN LANGUAGE/ART	10.0	10.0	.0
ECONOMICS	5.0	.0	5.0
ELECTIVES	75.0	15.0	60.0
TOTAL	225.0	106.0	119.0

STATE REQUIRED PROFICIENCY (BSA)
READING: PASS   MATH: FAIL
WRITING: PASS   SAMPLE: NT

GRADE POINT AVERAGES:

NON-AUGMENTED (10-12) 2.105
ELIGIBILITY (PER)   2.130

RANK: 178   CLASS SIZE: 429
GRADUATION DATE: NON GRADUATE

SEMESTERS CSF:

COURSE NAME	GR	CRED EARN	C T	C D		COURSE NAME	GR	CRED EARN	C T	C D
**BULLARD HIGH	9TH 94/95-02					PE/IND STUDY	C	3.5		S
KEYBRD/TYP +	F	.0		S		PHYS SCI P	C	10.0		S
ENGLISH IA P	F	.0		P		ACADEMIC GPA	1.625			
MATH A 1SEM	F	.0		P		**RESTART/TCW	10TH 96/97-04			
AUTO MECH I+	F	.0		S		ENGLISH II	N	.0		S
COED PE 9	B	.0		S		PE/IND STUDY	B	1.5		S
OFFICE SERV	B	5.0		S		MATH A	N	.0		S
ACADEMIC GPA	.000					US HISTORY P	N	.0		S
						SDC LIV	C	10.0		S
**PHILLIPPINES	10TH 95/96-04					ACADEMIC GPA	2.000			
CHRISTIAN LIVG	N	.0		S						
FILIPINO	B	10.0		S						
SOC STDIES I/II	B	5.0		S						
SOC STDIES I/II	C	5.0		S						
P E	C	10.0		S						
CHRISTIAN MORAL	N	.0		S						
ENGLISH	C	10.0		S						
SCI. (BIOLOGY)	C	10.0		S						
MATH (ALG. I)	C	10.0		S						
HOME EC	C	10.0		S						
ACADEMIC GPA	2.250									
**RESTART/TCW	10TH 96/97-02									
US HISTORY P	D	6.0		S						

CD: R=REPEATED CLASS, W=WAIVED CLASS, E=EXIT GRADE

OFFICIAL TRANSCRIPT SIGNED AND
SEALED BY: S. RICHARDSON

FORM LANDIN

25

13

```
                                    ID#: 333081  BIRTH: 1/26/79  SEX: F  | FATHER:                       MOTHER:                GUARDIAN:
                                    GR: 10  BDATE VERIFIED: AFFIDAVIT     | HORACIO                       SOLITA
FRESNO,        CA   93722           LEGAL NAME:                           | CURRENT SCHOOL: RESTART/TCW   SSN: 607-22-1783   BPLACE: FB

                            ATTENDANCE      GRADE    0    1    2    3    4    5    6    7    8    9    10   11   12

                                        EXCUSED                                                       6    1         5
                                        UNEXCUSED                                                     2    48   51
```

STUDENT ADDRESS LOG

ADDRESS	UNTIL

TRANSCRIPTS / RECORDS REQUESTED

DATE	SENT TO
8/11/99	CENTRAL ADULT SCH
5/21/96	PERSONAL (OFFICIAL)
4/26/95	PHILIPINES
12/08/94	JOHN MARSHALL
	H.S. L.A., CA
11/10/94	LOS ANGELES

SCHOOL LOG

```
D = DROPPED
E = ENROLLED
F = ENTERED FROM
T = TRANSFERRED TO
REASON LEFT:
ADULT EDUCATION
   DATE    SCHOOL                GR
T  5/08/97 ADULT ED             10
D  5/08/97 RESTART/TCW          10
E  9/11/96 RESTART/TCW          10
T  9/10/96 RESTART              11
D  9/10/96 BULLARD HIGH         11
E  8/26/96 BULLARD HIGH         11
T  4/26/95 PHILIPINES           09
D  4/26/95 BULLARD HIGH         09
F  1/04/95 LOS ANGELES
T 10/17/94 UNKNOWN
F  9/07/94 FORT MILLER
```

26

14

```
                      ID#: 333081   BIRTH: 1/26/79  SEX: F   | FATHER:                              GUARDIAN:
                      GR: 10  BDATE VERIFIED: AFFIDAVIT       |   HORACIO            MOTHER:
FRESNO,     CA  93722  LEGAL NAME:                            | CURRENT SCHOOL: RESTART/TCW    SOLITA    SSN: 6          BPLACE: F8
```

```
                    T E S T I N G    S C O R E S                          T E S T I N G    S C O R E S

TEST CD  DATE    TEST NAME          -------- SCORES --------    TEST CD  DATE    TEST NAME          -------- SCORES --------

BSA    T 08/94  READING             SS:159  PASS
                MATH                SS:129  FAIL
                WRITING SKILLS      SS:156  PASS

ITAS   05 05/91  READING COMPREHENSION       NP:57  NCE:54
                 TOTAL READING              NP:42  NCE:46
                 TOTAL LANGUAGE             NP:78  NCE:66
                 MATH APPLICATION/PROB  SLV  NP:28  NCE:38
                 TOTAL MATH                 NP:30  NCE:39
       06 05/92  READING COMPREHENSION       NP:46  NCE:48
                 TOTAL READING              NP:43  NCE:47
                 TOTAL LANGUAGE             NP:97  NCE:91
                 MATH APPLICATION/PROB  SLV  NP:35  NCE:42
                 TOTAL MATH                 NP:32  NCE:40
       07 05/93  READING COMPREHENSION       NP:32  NCE:40
                 TOTAL READING              NP:36  NCE:42
                 TOTAL LANGUAGE             NP:57  NCE:54
                 MATH APPLICATION/PROB  SLV  NP:36  NCE:42
                 TOTAL MATH                 NP:28  NCE:38
       08 05/94  READING COMPREHENSION       NP:50  NCE:50
                 TOTAL READING              NP:46  NCE:48
                 TOTAL LANGUAGE             NP:44  NCE:47
                 MATH APPLICATION/PROB  SLV  NP:23  NCE:35
                 TOTAL MATH                 NP:09  NCE:22

LPLANG   09/90  OTHER FILIPINO

LPSTAT   09/90  FEP-REDESIG 9/90-8/91
```

27

15

FRESNO UNIFIED SCHOOL DISTRICT - FRESNO, CALIFORNIA - PERMANENT RECORD FORM   CLASS OF 1999   PRINTED: 3/01/00 11:47 AM   PAGE:
** MIDDLE SCHOOL RECORD **

ID#: 333081   BIRTH: 1/26/79   SEX: F   FATHER: MOTHER: GUARDIAN:
GR: 10   BDATE VERIFIED: AFFIDAVIT   HORACIO   SOLITA
LEGAL NAME: CURRENT SCHOOL: RESTART/TCW   SSN: BPLACE: FB

FRESNO,   CA   93722

MIDDLE SCHOOL GRADE CODES: MIDDLE SCHOOL CITIZENSHIP:
A-EXCEPTIONALLY GOOD   G-GOOD
B-ABOVE AVERAGE   S-SATISFACTORY
C-AVERAGE   N-NEEDS IMPROVEMENT
D-BELOW AVERAGE
P-PASS   COURSE TITLE ABBREVIATIONS:
E-P.E. MEDICAL EXCUSE   B-BILINGUAL
F-FAILURE   G-GATE
WF-WITHDRAWAL WITH F   I-STRUCTURED ENGLISH IMMERSION
W-WITHDRAWAL   P-COLLEGE PREP
I-INCOMPLETE   S-SDAIE
                                 SDC-SPECIAL DAY CLASS

GRADE POINT AVERAGES:

CUMULATIVE (MID.SCH.) 2.000

IMMUNIZATIONS --
POLIO   06/27/89   08/11/89   02/28/9
DTP   06/27/89   08/11/89   02/28/9
MEASLES   06/27/89
MUMPS   06/27/89
RUBELLA   06/27/89
TB SKIN   08/03/89   RESULT: 15
CHEST X   08/03/89   RESULT: N

STATE REQUIRED PROFICIENCY (BSA)
READING: PASS   MATH: FAIL
WRITING: PASS   SAMPLE: NT

COURSE NAME	GR	CRED EARN	C T	C D
**FORT MILLER MID 7TH 92/93-01				
HMRM 7B				
EXPLD 7	C	5.0		S
COED P.E.	B	5.0		G
GEOG 7B	A	5.0		G
LANG 7B	A	5.0		G
MATH 7B	C	5.0		S
HLTH/L.S. 7B	B	5.0		G
ACADEMIC GPA	3.000			
**FORT MILLER MID 7TH 92/93-02				
HMRM 7B				
EXPLO 7		.0		S
COED P.E.	B	5.0		N
GEOG 7B	B	5.0		S
LANG 7B	A	5.0		S
MATH 7B	F	.0		S
HLTH/L.S. 7B	C	5.0		S
ACADEMIC GPA	2.500			
**FORT MILLER MID 7TH 92/93-03				
HMRM 7B				
PEER COUNS	A	5.0		G
COED P.E.	C	5.0		S

COURSE NAME	GR	CRED EARN	C T	C D
**FORT MILLER MID 7B				
WRLD HIST 7B	B	5.0		N
LANG 7B	C	5.0		S
MATH 7B	C	5.0		S
HLTH/L.S. 7B	C	5.0		S
ACADEMIC GPA	2.667			
**FORT MILLER MID 7TH 92/93-04				
HMRM 7B				
PEER COUNS		.0		G
COED P.E.	B	5.0		N
WRLD HIST 7B	C	5.0		S
LANG 7B	C	5.0		N
MATH 7B	D	5.0		S
HLTH/L.S. 7B	B	5.0		S
ACADEMIC GPA	2.333			
**FORT MILLER MID 8TH 93/94-01				
HR8B/7:55AM				
LASER LAB	A	5.0		S
COED.PE	B	5.0		G
U.S. HIST 8B	F	.0		S
LANG 8B	B	5.0		G
MATH 8B	C	5.0		G
SCI 8B	D	5.0		S

COURSE NAME	GR	CRED EARN	C T	C D
ACADEMIC GPA	2.167			
**FORT MILLER MID 8TH 93/94-02				
HR8B/7:55AM				
LASER LAB	A	5.0		
MANUFCTRNG 8	E	.0		N
COED PE	B	5.0		G
U.S. HIST 8B	C	5.0		G
LANG 8B	D	5.0		N
MATH 8B	C	5.0		N
SCI 8B	D	5.0		N
ACADEMIC GPA	2.167			
**FORT MILLER MID 8TH 93/94-03				
HR8B/7:55AM				
ART	C	.0		S
COED PE	F	.0		N
U.S. HIST 8B	B	5.0		N
LANG 8B	F	.0		S
MATH 8B	D	5.0		S
SCI 83	D	5.0		S
ACADEMIC GPA	.833			
**FORT MILLER MID 8TH 93/94-04				

COURSE NAME	GR	CRED EARN	C T	C D
HR8B/7:55AM				
ART	D	.0		S
COED PE	F	.0		N
U.S. HIST 8B	F	.0		S
LANG 8B	F	.0		S
MATH 8B	D	5.0		N
SCI 8B	D	5.0		N
ACADEMIC GPA	.333			
**FORT MILLER MID 8TH 93/94-SS				
HIST REV 8	N	.0		
ACADEMIC GPA	.000			

CD: R=REPEATED CLASS,   W=WAIVED CLASS,   E=EXIT GRADE

Name ▮▮▮ | Grade 6 YR Track

EXPLANATION OF TERMS

ACHIEVEMENT:
The quality of accomplishment compared to the District standard of expected student achievement for his/her grade level.

EFFORT:
The teacher's assessment of how the student applies himself/herself to the task.

DEFINITION OF MARKS

ACHIEVEMENT
- S Superior
- A Above Average
- C Average
- D Fulfillment of minimum requirements
- F Failure to meet minimum requirements
- — Not graded this period

EFFORT
- G Good
- S Satisfactory
- N Needs to Improve

	ACHIEVEMENT	FIRST QUARTER EFFORT	SECOND QUARTER ACHIEVEMENT	SECOND QUARTER EFFORT	THIRD QUARTER ACHIEVEMENT	THIRD QUARTER EFFORT	FOURTH QUARTER ACHIEVEMENT	FOURTH QUARTER EFFORT
LANGUAGE ARTS Reading Comprehension	C	S	C	S	C	S		
Oral Language*	C	S	C	S	C	S		
Written Language	C	S	B	S	C	S		
Spelling	C	S	C	C	B	S		
Handwriting	B	B	B	B	B	B		
MATHEMATICS	D	S	D	N	D	N		
SOCIAL STUDIES	B	S	C	N	C	N		
SCIENCE	X	X	X	B	X	X		
HEALTH	X	X	X	X	X	X		
PHYSICAL EDUCATION	X	N	X	S	X	S		
ART		D		N		N		
MUSIC								
INSTRUMENTAL MUSIC Band								
Orchestra								
ENGLISH LANGUAGE PROFICIENCY LEVEL, BSM I* (BSM Levels Range From 1-6) BSM II***								

CITIZENSHIP		Effort Only			
Conduct in Class	N	N	N		
Behavior on Playground	S	S	N		
Accepts Responsibility	N	N	N		

ATTENDANCE					
Days Absent	O	O	N		
Times Tardy	O	O	O		

*first grade students will have a parent conference for the first grading period, effort grades the second grading period, achievement and effort grades for the third and fourth grading periods.

For grades 1-3 only effort marks will be given for all reporting periods.

*Health/Science is marked two grading periods each year.

**For Limited English Students Only. - BSM I for Grades K-2/BSM II for 4-6
— Effort grades only are given in all Language Arts components until child reaches BSM Level 4
— In the other content areas students will receive achievement grades not later

Sign, Tear Off and Return to School

COMMENTS
Quarter 1 _Mr. ▮▮▮_

Check If Conference Requested ☐
SIGNATURE OF TEACHER

_▮▮▮_
Check If Conference Requested ☐
SIGNATURE OF PARENT OR GUARDIAN

Quarter 2 _Mr. ▮▮▮_

Check If Conference Requested ☐
SIGNATURE OF TEACHER

Check If Conference Requested ☐
SIGNATURE OF PARENT OR GUARDIAN

Quarter 3 _____

Check If Conference Requested ☐
SIGNATURE OF TEACHER

Check If Conference Requested ☐
SIGNATURE OF PARENT OR GUARDIAN

Quarter _____
Check If Conference Requested ☐
SIGNATURE OF PARENT OR GUARDIAN

Check If Conference Requested ☐
SIGNATURE OF TEACHER

Name ▮▮▮ Principal Mrs. Shepard Teacher Mr. Grossnicklaus Rm. 29 grade 6 school Del Mar School Year 19 91 - 19 92

TAB E
Respondent's Alcohol and Drug Counseling Diploma

DIPLOMA

PRESENTED TO

Has successfully completed a training course

Alcohol and Drug Counseling

at

ICDC COLLEGE

5422 Sunset Blvd.,
Hollywood, CA 90027

Revekka Gersher,
Executive Director

_11/02/11_
Date

Marina Frid,
Campus President, Hollywood Campus

11/02/11
Date

19

TAB F
Respondent's Parents U.S. Passports and Permanent Resident Cards

we the People

PASSPORT
PASSPORT
PASSAPORTE
USA

UNITED STATES OF AMERICA

P   USA   437486602

UNITED STATES OF AMERICA

Date of birth / Date de naissance / Fecha de nacimiento

12 Mar 1956

Place of birth / Lieu de naissance / Lugar de nacimiento

PHILIPPINES

Date of issue / Date de délivrance / Fecha de expedición

22 Feb 2008

Date of expiration / Date d'expiration / Fecha de caducidad

21 Feb 2018

Endorsements / Mentions Spéciales / Anotaciones

SEE PAGE 27

Sex / Sexe / Sexo

F

Authority / Autorité / Autoridad

United States
Department of State

USA

<<<<<<<<<<<<<<<<<<

437486502<9USA5603129F1802212227297977<210290

21

TAB G
Respondent's Siblings U.S. Passports and Permanent Resident Cards

LOS IR2

WAIVED

092575

36

24

THE UNITED STATES OF AMERICA

DEPARTMENT OF

No. 30773772

NATURALIZATION

USCIS Registration No.: A45907649

Personal description of Holder as of date of issuance of this Certificate:

Date of Birth: OCTOBER 29, 1981

Sex: MALE

Height: 5 *Feet* 6 *inches*

Marital status: MARRIED

Country of former nationality: PHILIPPINES

(Complete and true signature of holder)

Be it known that ████████

residing at ████████

having applied to the Director, U.S. Citizenship and Immigration Services for placement of a Certificate of Naturalization and having proved to the satisfaction of the Director that (s)he

COMPLIED WITH THE APPLICABLE PROVISIONS OF SUCH NATURALIZATION AND WAS ENTITLED TO BE ADMITTED TO CITIZENSHIP SUCH PERSON HAVING TAKEN THE OATH OF ALLEGIANCE IN A CEREMONY CONDUCTED BY THE U.S. DISTRICT COURT CENTRAL DISTRICT

AT POMONA, CALIFORNIA ON OCTOBER 24, 2007

Now Therefore, in pursuance of the authority contained in Section 343 ( ) of the Immigration and Nationality Act, this Certificate of Naturalization is issued.

this 26TH *day of* NOVEMBER 2013 *and the seal of the Department of Homeland Security affixed pursuant to statute.*

U. S. Citizenship and Immigration Services

1675890

I certify that the description given is true, and that the photograph affixed hereto is a likeness of me.

25

TAB H
Respondent's ASC
Appointment Notice

THIS NOTICE DOES NOT GRANT ANY IMMIGRATION STATUS OR BENEFIT.

ASC Appointment Notice	APPLICATION/PETITION/REQUEST NUMBER SRC1423750478		NOTICE DATE 09/05/2014
CASE TYPE I485 - APPLICATION TO REGISTER PERMANENT RESIDENCE OR ADJUST STATUS	SOCIAL SECURITY NUMBER	USCIS A# A042049242	CODE 3
ACCOUNT NUMBER	TCR	SERVICE CENTER TSC	PAGE 1 of 1

c/o CHRISTOPHER A REED
LAW OFFICES OF BRIAN D LERNER
3233 E BROADWAY
LONG BEACH CA 90803

To process your application, petition, or request, the U. S. Citizenship & Immigration Services (USCIS) must capture your biometrics.
**PLEASE APPEAR AT THE BELOW APPLICATION SUPPORT CENTER AT THE DATE AND TIME SPECIFIED.
IF YOU FAIL TO APPEAR AS SCHEDULED, YOUR APPLICATION, PETITION, OR REQUEST WILL BE CONSIDERED ABANDONED.**

APPLICATION SUPPORT CENTER USCIS WILSHIRE 1015 WILSHIRE BOULEVARD 1ST FLOOR, SUITE 100 LOS ANGELES CA 90017	PLEASE READ THIS ENTIRE NOTICE CAREFULLY. DATE AND TIME OF APPOINTMENT 09/23/2014 03:00PM

WHEN YOU GO TO THE APPLICATION SUPPORT CENTER TO HAVE YOUR BIOMETRICS TAKEN, YOU MUST BRING:
1. THIS APPOINTMENT NOTICE and
2. PHOTO IDENTIFICATION. Naturalization applicants must bring their Alien Resident Card. All other applicants must bring a passport, driver's license, national ID, military ID, or State-issued photo ID. If you appear without proper identification, you will not be fingerprinted.

CELL PHONES, CAMERAS, OR OTHER RECORDING DEVICES ARE NOT PERMITTED.

REQUEST FOR RESCHEDULING

❑ Please reschedule my appointment. Once USCIS receives your request, you will be sent a new appointment notice. Make a copy of this notice for your records, then mail the original with your request to BPU, Alexandria ASC, Suite 100, 8850 Richmond Hwy, Alexandria, VA 22309-1586

APPLICATION NUMBER
I485 - SRC1423750478

If you have any questions regarding this notice, please call 1-800-375-5283.

WARNING: *Due to limited seating availability in our lobby area, only persons who are necessary to assist with transportation or completing the biometrics worksheet should accompany you. If you have open wounds or bandages/casts when you appear, the USCIS may reschedule your appointment if it is determined your injuries will interfere with taking your biometrics.*

Please see the back of this notice for important information.

TAB I
Respondent's California Criminal History Information (CALDOJ)

KAMALA D. HARRIS
Attorney General

State of California
DEPARTMENT OF JUSTICE

BUREAU OF CRIMINAL INFORMATION AND ANALYSIS
P.O. Box 903417
SACRAMENTO, CA 94203-4170

August 19, 2014

RE: California Criminal History Information

Dear Applicant:

This is in response to your record review request concerning the existence of a California criminal history record maintained in the files of the Department of Justice's Bureau of Criminal Information and Analysis. Your fingerprints did identify to an existing California criminal history record and a copy of that record is enclosed. If you wish to challenge the accuracy or completeness of your record, please complete and return the enclosed form (BCIA 8706) and supporting documentation to the address noted above. As requested, a copy of this record review response has been sent to your designee.

Pursuant to California Penal Code section 11121, the purpose of a record review request is to afford an individual with a copy of their record and to refute any erroneous or inaccurate information contained therein. The intent is not to be used for licensing, certification or employment purposes.

Additionally, California Penal Code sections 11125, 11142, and 11143 does not allow for a person or agency to make a request to another person to provide them with a copy of an individual's criminal history or notification that a record does not exist; does not allow an authorized person to furnish the record to an unauthorized person; nor does it allow an unauthorized person to buy, receive or possess the record or information. A violation of these section codes is a misdemeanor.

Sincerely,

Cindy Santos

Record Review Unit
Applicant Information and Certification Program
Bureau of Criminal Information and Analysis

For KAMALA D. HARRIS
Attorney General

Enclosures
BCIA 8711d (Rev. 08/13)

29

****
FOR CALIFORNIA AGENCIES ONLY - HAS PREVIOUS QUALIFYING OFFENSE. COLLECT
DNA IF INCARCERATED, CONFINED, OR ON PROBATION OR PAROLE FOLLOWING ANY
MISDEMEANOR OR FELONY CONVICTION. REQUEST KITS AND INFO AT (510) 620-
3300 OR PC296.PC296@DOJ.CA.GOV.
****
** PALM PRINT ON FILE AT DOJ FOR ADDITIONAL INFORMATION PLEASE E-MAIL
PALM.PRINT@DOJ.CA.GOV
** III CALIFORNIA ONLY SOURCE RECORD
CII/A28402571
DOB/19790126   SEX/F RAC/HISPANIC
HGT/500 WGT/100 EYE/BRO HAI/BRO POB/PI
CTZ/PHILIPPINES
NAM/001 UNLAYAO,ANNA CARISSA

FBI/679551RC6
DMV/B7612926
SOC/607221783
SMT/TAT BACK-UNKNOWN   ; TAT L ANKL-UNKNOWN   ;
    TAT R SHLD-UNKNOWN
* * * *

ARR/DET/CITE: NAM:001 DOB:19790126
20070602   CAPD FRESNO

CNT:001   #0766634-428787
  470(D) PC-FALSE CHECKS/RECORDS/CERTS/ETC   TOC:F
    SCN:S49A1530023
- - - -
COURT: NAM:001
20070724   CASC FRESNO CENTRAL

CNT:001   #F107904397
  470(D) PC-FALSE CHECKS/RECORDS/CERTS/ETC   TOC:F
 DISPO:DISMISSED

CNT:002
  530.5(A) PC-GET CREDIT/ETC:USE OTHER'S ID   TOC:F
 DISPO:DISMISSED

CNT:003
  496(A) PC-RECEIVE/ETC KNOWN STOLEN PROPERTY   TOC:F
 DISPO:DISMISSED

CNT:004
  484E(D) PC-USE ACCESS ACCOUNT INFO W/O CONSENT   TOC:F
*DISPO:CONVICTED
  CONV STATUS:MISDEMEANOR PER 17PC
   SEN: 036 MONTHS PROBATION, 003 DAYS JAIL, 003 DAYS JAIL OR FINE,
       FINE, RESTN

 DISPO:CONVICTION CERT BY CLERK OF THE COURT
 DISPO:FOR CERT INFO SEE AUTOMATED ARCHIVE SYS

20081229
 DISPO:EARLY DISMISSAL FROM PROBATION
* * * *

ARR/DET/CITE: NAM:001 DOB:19790126

30

```
20080325    CAPD FRESNO        (---)

CNT:001      #0886809-4287b.
  11377(A) HS-POSSESS CONTROLLED SUBSTANCE                      TOC:F


CNT:002                                                         TOC:M
  11550(A) HS-USE/UNDER INFL CONTRLD SUBSTANCE
  SCN:S49B0850009
- - - -
COURT:              NAM:001
20080514  CASC FRESNO CENTRAL

CNT:001      #F08902017                                         TOC:M
  11550(A) HS-USE/UNDER INFL CONTRLD SUBSTANCE
  DISPO:DISMISSED


CNT:002                                                         TOC:F
  11377(A) HS-POSSESS CONTROLLED SUBSTANCE
  DISPO:PROC SUSP/DRUG CRT-DEFERRED JUDGEMENT


20081229
  DISPO:DRG CRT/DEFER JDGMNT-TRM CRM PROC REINST
- - - -
COURT:              NAM:001
20081229  CASC FRESNO CENTRAL

CNT:001      #F08902017                                         TOC:F
  11377(A) HS-POSSESS CONTROLLED SUBSTANCE
*DISPO:CONVICTED
  CONV STATUS:FELONY
    SEN: 024 MONTHS PROBATION, 002 DAYS JAIL, WORK PROGRAM, IMP SEN SS

  DISPO:COND OF PROB-DRUG TREATMENT PLACEMENT
* * * *

ARR/DET/CITE:        NAM:001  DOB:19790126
20081201  CAPD FRESNO

CNT:001      #08103848-428787                                  TOC:F
  11377(A) HS-POSSESS CONTROLLED SUBSTANCE


CNT:002                                                         TOC:M
  11364 HS-POSSESS CONTROL SUBSTANCE PARAPHERNA


CNT:003                                                         TOC:F
  12316(B)(1) PC-PROHIBITED OWN/ETC AMMO/ETC
    ADR:20081201 (200,LOMA, ,S,LA,CA,90026)
    SCN:S49B3360019
- - - -
COURT:              NAM:001
20081229  CASC FRESNO CENTRAL

CNT:001      #F08907500
  11364 HS-POSSESS CONTROL SUBSTANCE PARAPHERNA
  DISPO:DISMISSED


CNT:002
  11377(A) HS-POSSESS CONTROLLED SUBSTANCE
*DISPO:CONVICTED
  CONV STATUS:FELONY
    SEN: 024 MONTHS PROBATION, 001 DAYS JAIL, WORK PROGRAM, IMP SEN SS

  DISPO:COND OF PROB-DRUG TREATMENT PLACEMENT
  DISPO:CONVICTION CERT BY CLERK OF THE COURT
```

DISPO:FOR CERT INFO SE[...]TOMATED ARCHIVE SYS
  *   *   *   END . MESSAGE   *   *   *

TAB J
Docket Sheet – F07904397

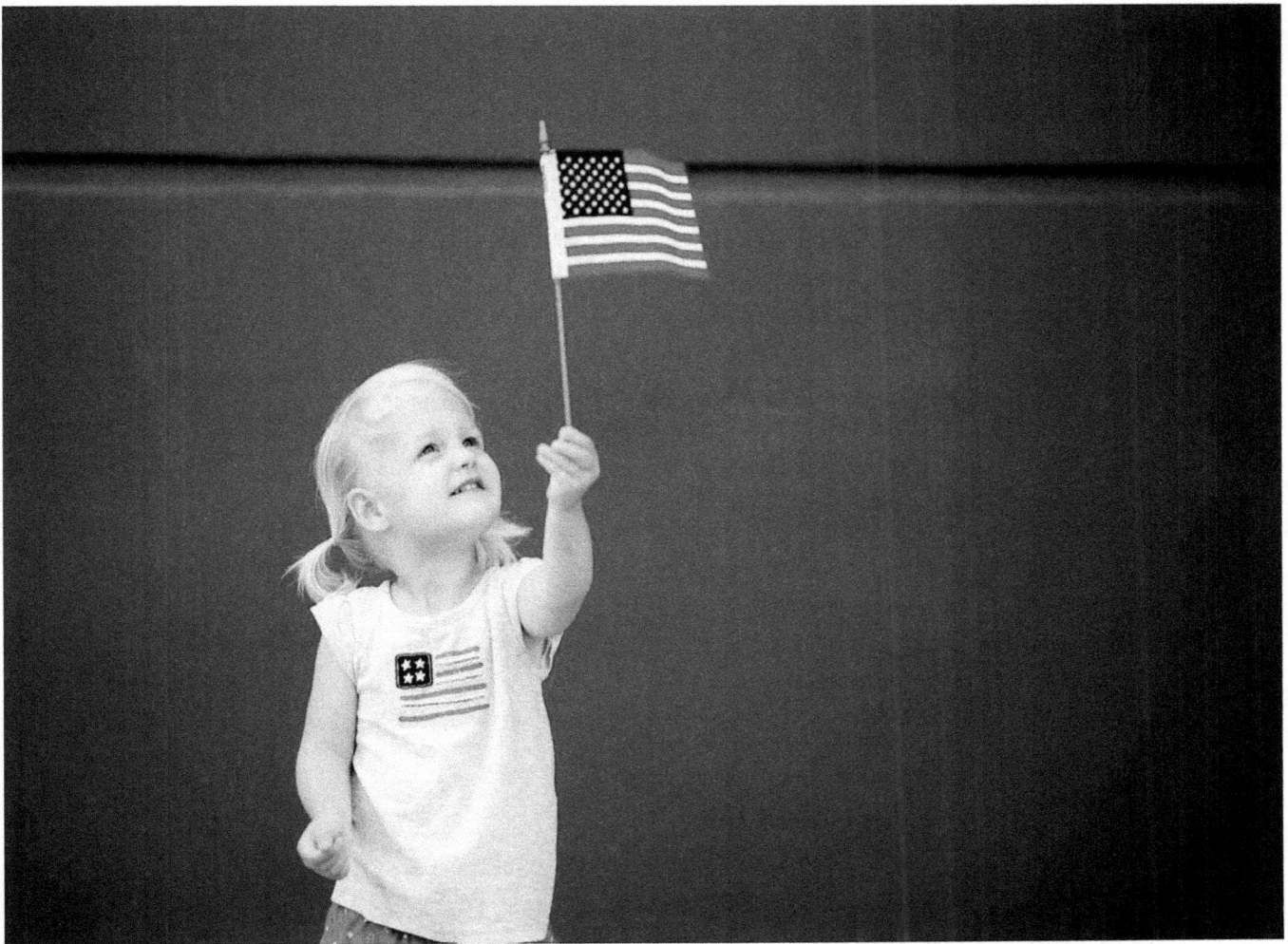

DOCKET REPORT

Case : F07904397 F A

Name : Unlayao, Anna Carissa Estaya

Date of Action	Seq Nbr	Code	Text
06/05/07			
	1	FLDOC	**Original Complaint filed by District Attorney.**
	2	FLNAM	Name filed: ███████████
	3	FLCNT	FELONY charge of 470(d) PC filed as count 1. Date of violation: 06/02/2007.
	4	FLCNT	FELONY charge of 484e(d) PC filed as count 2. Date of violation: 06/02/2007.
	5	FLCNT	FELONY charge of 530.5(a) PC filed as count 3. Date of violation: 06/02/2007.
	6	FLCNT	FELONY charge of 496(a) PC filed as count 4. Date of violation: 06/02/2007.
	7	JLINC	Defendant is in custody at the Fresno County Jail.
	8	BLSET	Court orders bail set in the amount of $47, 000.00.
	9	COJUS	Clerk's office filed JUS8715 form.
06/06/07			
	1	CLADD	**Case calendared on 06/06/07 at 01:30 PM in Department 32, Add-on for Arraignment Initial Appearance.**
	2	HHELD	**Hearing held on 6/6/2007 at 01:30:00 PM in Department 32, Add-on for Arraignment Initial Appearance.**
	3	OFJUD	Judicial Officer: Gottlieb, David, Judge
	4	OFJA	Courtroom Clerk: Gonzales, Tricia
	5	OFREP	Court Reporter: Zoanne Williams
	6	APDDA	People present and are represented by, Ryan McGinthy, Deputy District Attorney.
	7	CLSET2	**Arraignment re: Continued Arraignment set on 06/07/2007 at 08:30 AM in Department 32, Add-on.**
	8	TEXT	Cont. to check custody status
	9	DSCSR	**Defendant remains in custody.**
	10	OFMCD	Minutes of T. Gonzales entered by Delia A on 06/06/2007.
	11	NTJAL	Notice to Sheriff issued.
	12	HHELD	**Hearing held on 6/6/2007 at 01:30:00 PM in Department 32, Add-on for Arraignment Initial Appearance.**
	13	OFJUD	Judicial Officer: ^1^, ^2^
	14	OFJA	Courtroom Clerk: ^1^
	15	OFREP	Court Reporter: ^1^

DOCKET REPORT

Case: F07904397 F A

Name: ████████████████

Date of Action	Seq Nbr	Code	Text
06/07/07			
	1	FLCRT	Original charging document filed at 1100 Van Ness Avenue^Fresno, CA 93724 USA
	2	HHELD	**Hearing held on 6/7/2007 at 08:30:00 AM in Department 32, Add-on for Arraignment Continued Arraignment.**
	3	OFJUD	Judicial Officer: Gottlieb, David, Judge
	4	OFJA	Courtroom Clerk: Gonzales, Tricia
	5	OFREP	Court Reporter: Williams, Zoanne
	6	APDDA	People present and are represented by, Samuel A Luton, Deputy District Attorney.
	7	JLTXT	**Per deputy, deft. not I/C**
	8	CODFA	Court orders District Attorney to file affidavit in support of arrest warrant.
	9	OFMCD	Minutes of T. Gonzales entered by Delia A on 06/07/2007.
	10	NTJAL	Notice to Sheriff issued.
06/08/07			
	1	TEXT	Surety Bond posted 6/5/07, no Affidavit in support of arrest warrant needed. Deft. to appear 6/18/07 for Arrn.
	2	BBPST	Bail Bond Number LG5-523993 posted in the amount of $2000.00 by ALADDINBB of LGISU.
	3	CLSET2	**Arraignment re: Initial Appearance set on 06/18/2007 at 08:30 AM in Department 32, 3rd Floor.**
06/18/07			
	1	HHELD	**Hearing held on 6/18/2007 at 08:30:00 AM in Department 32, 3rd Floor for Arraignment Initial Appearance.**
	2	OFJUD	Judicial Officer: Gottlieb, David, Judge
	3	OFJA	Courtroom Clerk: Gonzales, Tricia
	4	OFREP	Court Reporter: Gonzales, Valerie
	5	APDDA	People present and are represented by, Ryan McGinthy, Deputy District Attorney.
	6	COCCW	Case having been called at 08:58 AM. Defendant not present.
	7	WAISD	**Bench warrant ordered issued for defendant. Bail set at $40,000.00, Bailable. Night service: Yes**
	8	WAWSD	Bench warrant issued by David Gottlieb.
	9	BLBFN	Court orders bail bond # LG5-523993 FORFEITED.
	10	OFMCD	Minutes of T. Gonzales entered by Delia A on 06/18/2007.

DOCKET REPORT

Case : F07904397 F A

Name : ████████████████

Date of Action	Seq Nbr	Code	Text
06/19/07			
	1	CLCST2	Defendant at counter to set Failure to Appear re: Arraignment set on 07/09/2007 at 08:30 AM in Department CRIM-B102.
	2	FIRAB	Letter of reassumption of surety bond filed.
07/09/07			
	1	CLCAN	FTA ARGN set on 07/09/07 at 08:30 AM in B102 has been cancelled.
	2	CLADD	Case calendared on 07/09/07 at 08:30 AM in Department 32, 3rd Floor for FTA Arraignment.
	3	HHELD	Hearing held on 7/9/2007 at 08:30:00 AM in Department 32, 3rd Floor for Failure to Appear Arraignment.
	4	OFJUD	Judicial Officer: Gottlieb, David, Judge
	5	OFJA	Courtroom Clerk: Gonzales, Tricia
	6	OFREP	Court Reporter: Lucy Blevins
	7	APDPD	Court appoints Public Defender to represent Defendant.
	8	APPDD	Public Defender Marina P Pincus appearing with defendant.
	9	APDDA	People present and are represented by, P Cheong, Deputy District Attorney.
	10	DFCRC	Copy of Complaint given to Defendant.
	11	ADWRA	The defendant waives reading of the complaining document, waives formal arraignment and waives reading of constitutional and statutory rights.
	12	PLNGA	Defendant waives reading of the Original Complaint, constitutional and statutory rights NG not guilty to all counts.
	13	WVTIM	Defendant waives statutory time for Preliminary Hearing.
	14	WVTGN	Defendant enters general time waiver. 10/60
	15	CLSET2	Pre Prelim re: Pre Prelim set on 07/24/2007 at 08:30 AM in Department 32, 3rd Floor.
	16	DSOTBP	Defendant is ordered to be present at next hearing.
	17	WAREC	Warrant issued on 06/18/2007 ordered recalled for defendant.
	18	JLTXT	Surety Bond reinstatement letter filed.
	19	SVBBFF	Court orders bail bond forfeiture for bond # LG5-523993 vacated. Bond ordered reinstated.
	20	DSCSR	Defendant remains surety bond.

DOCKET REPORT / ALL CATEGORIES
Unlayao, Anna Carissa Estaya - F07904397

9/2/14 11:38 am

36

DOCKET REPORT

Case : F07904397 F A

Name : ▒▒▒▒▒▒▒▒▒▒▒▒▒▒▒▒

Date of Action	Seq Nbr	Code	Text
07/09/07			
	21	OFMCD	Minutes of T. GONZALES entered by A LY on 07/09/2007.
07/24/07			
	1	HHELD	**Hearing held on 7/24/2007 at 08:30:00 AM in Department 32, 3rd Floor for Pre Prelim Pre Prelim.**
	2	OFJUD	Judicial Officer: Gottlieb, David, Judge
	3	OFJA	Courtroom Clerk: Gonzales, Tricia
	4	OFREP	Court Reporter: Oftedal, Lupe
	5	APPDD	Public Defender Todd D Eilers appearing with defendant.
	6	APDDA	People present and are represented by, Ed Browne, Deputy District Attorney.
	7	CT17B	Pursuant to Section 17 of the Penal Code, with approval of the Court and consent of the defendant, and by stipulation of counsel, this Court determines that the offense alleged in the complaint, Count 2, 484e(d) PC, is a misdemeanor, and further, that this case shall proceed as if the defenant has been arraigned on a misdemeanor complaint.
	8	PLWDA	Defendant motions to withdraw plea.
	9	PLWTH	**Defendant's motion to WITHDRAW NOT GUILTY PLEA to count(s) 2 granted.**
	10	PLNCT	**Defendant waives reading of the Original Complaint constitutional and statutory rights. NOLO CONTENDERE as to count(s) 2. Court finds there is factual basis for the plea and accepts the Nolo Contendere plea.**
	11	FICOP	The change of plea form is signed and filed in open court. Court accepts the plea and finds it was made knowingly, intelligently and voluntarily and that the plea is supported by a factual basis (People v West).
	12	DFADV	Defendant advised of rights in open court.
	13	CDCDM	Count(s) 1, 3, 4 DISMISSED - Other reason.
	14	WVFALC	Defendant waives time and formal arraignment for judgment and sentencing and states there is no legal cause why judgment should not be pronounced.
	15	WVTFS	The defendant waives statutory time for sentencing.
	16	PBGRT	The Court grants probation.
	17	PRISS	Imposition of judgment and sentence is suspended for a period of 3 Years and defendant is placed on 3 Years CONDITIONAL SENTENCE probation for count(s) 2 on the following terms and conditions as ordered by the Court:

DOCKET REPORT

Case : F07904397 F A

Name : ████████████████

Date of Action	Seq Nbr	Code	Text
07/24/07			
	18	SEJAL	As to count(s) 2, defendant to serve 40 Days Fresno County Jail.
	19	JLSTA	Court grants jail stay until 11/02/2007 at 07:00 PM, Fresno County Jail.
	20	DFRTP	Defendant referred to Adult Offender Work Program.
	21	COACT	Report to the ACTION Center as directed by the court.
	22	JLCTS1	Credit for time served 3, actual 3, goodtime/worktime 0, treatment 0.
	23	SEFIN2	As to count(s) 2, pay a FINE of $470.00.
	24	SESEC	Pursuant to Penal Code 1465.8, a Court Security Fee is owed to the Court and included in the current balance.
	25	SEFEE	Pay FEE of $100.00 Restitution Fund PC 1202.4.
	26	ADATC	Pursuant to Penal Code 1202.44, defendant advised that if Probation is revoked an additional $100.00 will be ordered.
	27	STPYS	Payments to be paid at the rate of $35.00 per month beginning 09/04/2007 and on the 4 of each month thereafter until paid in full. $35.00 installment fee will be added to balance of fine.
	28	PROBY	Obey all laws.
	29	PRDIR	Defendant to obey all orders of the Probation Officer and report as directed.
	30	PRSAS	Submit to search and seizure of your person, residence, vehicle or any property under your control at any time of the day or night by any law enforcement or probation officer with or without a warrant, and with or without reasonable cause or reasonable suspicion.
	31	PRCHA	Report change of address to the Court and/or Probation within 7 days.
	32	PRDRG	Do not use drugs.
	33	PRNCC	Do not possess any checking account or fictitious writing instruments without the permission of the Probation Officer or the Court.
	34	TEXT	Or any ficticious writing instruments
	35	PRPRP	Defendant not to possess unlawful property.
	36	DSRFC	Defendant released on probation.
	37	BLBXN	Court orders surety bond # LG5-523993 exonerated.
	38	OFMCD	Minutes of T. Gonzales entered by Delia A on 07/24/2007.

██████████████ - F07904397

DOCKET REPORT

Case : F07904397 F A

Name : ███████████████

Date of Action	Seq Nbr	Code	Text
07/25/07	1	BLBBNS	Bail Bond Notice Bail Bond Exoneration Sent for Bond # LG5-523993
08/10/07	1	COJUS	Clerk's office mailed JUS8715 form.
09/18/07	1	WCFTPW	Defendant has failed to pay, case to be reviewed for failure to pay action.
09/19/07	1	WCPDN	Defendant failed to pay, warning letter sent.
10/02/07	1	REMRC	Remittance from receipt # 1186331 received in the amount of $ 35.00.
11/05/07	1	WCFTP	Initiate FTP action identification.
11/06/07	1	WCPWQ	Schedule case for potential warrant work queue - FTP Not Hold Eligible
11/22/07	1	NTSNT	Courtesy Notice - FTP letter sent.
02/19/08	1	CLSET2	**Probation Hearing re: Modification set on 03/10/2008 at 01:30 PM in Department 11, B1 Floor.**
03/10/08	1	MOTION	Motion taken off calendar set in error to Dept. 11.
	2	HHELD	**Hearing held on 03/10/2008 at 01:30 AM in Department 11, B1 Floor for Probation Hearing Modification.**
	3	OFJUD	Judicial Officer: W Kent Hamlin, Judge
	4	OFJA	Courtroom Clerk: G. Broome
	5	OFREP	Court Reporter: Noelle Acosta
	6	CLOFF	Case taken off calendar.
	7	TEXT	Case set in wrong department. No appearance by defendant. Case taken off calendar, no action taken.
04/04/08	1	FIRPT	Report filed from AOWP.

DOCKET REPORT

Case : F07904397 F A

Name :

Date of Action	Seq Nbr	Code	Text
04/04/08			
	2	COFFJ	Clerk's Office forwards case to Judicial Officer Alvin Harrell for consideration. FTA/AOWP.
04/08/08			
	1	JLWARR	Jail Warrant issued. Defendant to serve 25 days in Fresno County Jail.
12/09/08			
	1	CLSET2	**Probation Hearing re: VOP Arraignment set on 12/10/2008 at 08:30 AM in Department 33, 3rd Floor.**
	2	TEXT	Per request of DA
12/10/08			
	1	HHELD	**Hearing held on 12/10/2008 at 08:30:00 AM in Department 33, 3rd Floor for Probation Hearing VOP Arraignment.**
	2	OFJUD	Judicial Officer: Whitehead, Denise, Judge
	3	OFJA	Courtroom Clerk: Lawson, Ginger
	4	OFREP	Court Reporter: Oftedal, Lupe
	5	APPDD	Public Defender Mari Anita Torres appearing with defendant.
	6	APDDA	People present and are represented by, Greg Strickland, Deputy District Attorney.
	7	JLTXT	**Per Jail records defendant is serving time on jail warrant (no bail) until 12/25/08**
	8	CLSET2	**Hearing re: For Reference Only set on 12/29/2008 at 08:30 AM in Department 33, 3rd Floor.**
	9	DSOTBP	Defendant is ordered to be present at next hearing.
	10	DSCSR	**Defendant remains in custody.**
	11	OFMCD	Minutes of G.Lawson entered by L.Embrey on 12/10/2008.
	12	NTJAL	Notice to Sheriff issued.
12/29/08			
	1	HHELD	**Hearing held on 12/29/2008 at 08:30:00 AM in Department 33, 3rd Floor for Hearing For Reference Only.**
	2	OFJUD	Judicial Officer: Whitehead, Denise, Judge
	3	OFJA	Courtroom Clerk: Lawson, Ginger
	4	OFREP	Court Reporter: Loring, Catherine
	5	APPDD	Public Defender Mari Anita Torres appearing with defendant.

DOCKET REPORT

Case : F07904397 F A

Name :

Date of Action	Seq Nbr	Code	Text
12/29/08			
	6	APDDA	People present and are represented by, Scott Sanders, Deputy District Attorney.
	7	APBOT	Probation Officer, present in court. K. Davis.
	8	COCTR	Court orders this case to trail case F08907500.
	9	PBTCR	Court orders probation reinstated, same terms and conditions.
	10	PBMOD	Conditional Probation modified as follows:
	11	PRRJR	The Court reserves jurisdiction over the Issue of restitution to be paid to victim(s).
	12	PBTRM	Court orders probation terminated as to count(s) 2.
	13	DSRFC	Defendant released on all counts.
	14	OFMCD	Minutes of G.Lawson entered by L.Embrey on 12/29/2008.
	15	COSUB	Clerk's office sends JUS8715 subsequent action form to the Department of Justice.
01/14/13			
	1	WAFTP	Defendant failed to pay fine on 10/04/2007. Failure to Pay hold issued.
01/15/13			
	1	GCSER	Case Sent to Collections

copy of the original on file in this office.

ATTEST: SEP 02 2014

State of California, County of Fresno

By _____ , Deputy

Superior Court Clerk,

Brian D. Lerner (Bar No. 158536)
Christopher A. Reed (Bar No. 235438)
Law Offices of Brian D. Lerner, APC
3233 E. Broadway
Long Beach, California 90803
Telephone: (562) 495-0554
Facsimile: (562) 608-8672

Attorneys for Respondent

UNITED STATES DEPARTMENT OF JUSTICE

EXECUTIVE OFFICE FOR IMMIGRATION REVIEW

IMMIGRATION COURT

LOS ANGELES, CALIFORNIA

In the Matter of:

███████████████████   File No: ████████████

Respondent,

In Removal Proceedings.

Immigration Judge: Monica Little   Next Hearing: October 27, 2016 at 1:00 p.m.

SUPPLEMENTAL DOCUMENTS FOR APPLICATION FOR CANCELLATION OF REMOVAL FOR CERTAIN PERMANENT RESIDENTS

TABLE OF CONTENTS

TAB K
Respondent's Daughters' Birth Certificate

STATE OF CALIFORNIA
CERTIFICATION OF VITAL RECORD

COUNTY of FRESNO
DEPARTMENT OF PUBLIC HEALTH
FRESNO, CALIFORNIA

CERTIFICATE OF LIVE BIRTH
STATE OF CALIFORNIA
USE BLACK INK ONLY

1201510008760

STATE FILE NUMBER		LOCAL REGISTRATION NUMBER

THIS CHILD

1A. NAME OF CHILD - FIRST	1B. MIDDLE	1C. LAST
▮		

2. SEX	3A. THIS BIRTH, SINGLE, TWIN, ETC.	3B. IF MULTIPLE, THIS CHILD 1ST, 2ND, ETC.	4A. DATE OF BIRTH - MM/DD/CCYY	4B. HOUR - 24 HOUR CLOCK TIME
FEMALE	SINGLE	-	07/11/2015	1320

PLACE OF BIRTH

5A. PLACE OF BIRTH - NAME OF HOSPITAL OR FACILITY	5B. STREET ADDRESS - STREET AND NUMBER, OR LOCATION
CLOVIS COMMUNITY HOSPITAL	

5C. CITY	5D. COUNTY
CLOVIS	FRESNO

FATHER/PARENT

6A. NAME OF FATHER/PARENT - FIRST	6B. MIDDLE	6C. LAST	7. BIRTHPLACE - STATE/COUNTRY	8. DATE OF BIRTH - MM/DD/CCYY
-	-	-		

MOTHER/PARENT

9A. NAME OF MOTHER/PARENT - FIRST	9B. MIDDLE	9C. LAST - BIRTH NAME	10. BIRTHPLACE - STATE/COUNTRY	11. DATE OF BIRTH - MM/DD/CCYY
▮	▮	▮	PHILIPPINES	01/26/1979

INFORMANT AND BIRTH CERTIFICATION

I CERTIFY THAT I HAVE REVIEWED THE STATED INFORMATION AND THAT IT IS TRUE AND CORRECT TO THE BEST OF MY KNOWLEDGE.	12A. PARENT OR OTHER INFORMANT - SIGNATURE	12B. RELATIONSHIP TO CHILD	12C. DATE SIGNED - MM/DD/CCYY
		MOTHER	07/14/2015

I CERTIFY THAT THE CHILD WAS BORN ALIVE AT THE DATE, HOUR, AND PLACE STATED.	13A. ATTENDANT/CERTIFIER - SIGNATURE AND DEGREE OR TITLE	13B. LICENSE NUMBER	13C. DATE SIGNED - MM/DD/CCYY
	A. Clark, Birth Clerk	A350410	07/14/2015

13D. TYPED NAME, TITLE AND MAILING ADDRESS OF ATTENDANT	14. TYPED NAME AND TITLE OF CERTIFIER IF OTHER THAN ATTENDANT
GOPAL R GADE, MD, 6183 N FRESNO #105, FRESNO	A. CLARK, BIRTH CLERK

LOCAL REGISTRAR

15A. DATE OF DEATH - MM/DD/CCYY	15B. STATE FILE NO. - STATE USE ONLY	16. LOCAL REGISTRAR - SIGNATURE	17. DATE ACCEPTED FOR REGISTRATION - MM/DD/CCYY
		KENNETH BIRD, M.D.	07/22/2015

CERTIFIED COPY OF VITAL RECORDS
STATE OF CALIFORNIA, COUNTY OF FRESNO

This is a true and exact reproduction of the document officially registered and placed on file in the Vital Records Section, Fresno Co. Department of Public Health.

001143418

DATE ISSUED MAY 31 2016

COUNTY HEALTH OFFICER
REGISTRAR OF VITAL STATISTICS

This copy not valid unless prepared on engraved border displaying date, seal and signature of Registrar

57

42

TAB L
Proof of Biometrics

Department of Homeland Security
U.S. Citizenship and Immigration Ser~

rm I-797C, Notice of Action

THIS NOTICE DOES NOT GRANT ANY IMMIGRATION STATUS OR BENEFIT.

ASC Appointment Notice	APPLICATION/PETITION/REQUEST NUMBER SRC1423750478		NOTICE DATE 09/05/2014
CASE TYPE I485 - APPLICATION TO REGISTER PERMANENT RESIDENCE OR ADJUST STATUS	SOCIAL SECURITY NUMBER	USCIS A# A042049242	CODE 3
ACCOUNT NUMBER	TCR	SERVICE CENTER TSC	PAGE 1 of 1

C/O EUIR 42A
200 S LOMA DR 3
LOS ANGELES CA 90026

To process your application, petition, or request, the U. S. Citizenship & Immigration Services (USCIS) must capture your biometrics.
PLEASE APPEAR AT THE BELOW APPLICATION SUPPORT CENTER AT THE DATE AND TIME SPECIFIED.
IF YOU FAIL TO APPEAR AS SCHEDULED, YOUR APPLICATION, PETITION, OR REQUEST WILL BE CONSIDERED ABANDONED.

APPLICATION SUPPORT CENTER USCIS WILSHIRE 1015 WILSHIRE BOULEVARD 1ST FLOOR, SUITE 100 LOS ANGELES CA 90017	PLEASE READ THIS ENTIRE NOTICE CAREFULLY. DATE AND TIME OF APPOINTMENT 09/23/2014 03:00PM

WHEN YOU GO TO THE APPLICATION SUPPORT CENTER TO HAVE YOUR BIOMETRICS TAKEN, YOU MUST BRING:
1. THIS APPOINTMENT NOTICE and
2. PHOTO IDENTIFICATION. Naturalization applicants must bring their Alien Resident Card. All other applicants must bring a passport, driver's license, national ID, military ID, or State-issued photo ID. If you appear without proper identification, you will not be fingerprinted.

CELL PHONES, CAMERAS, OR OTHER RECORDING DEVICES ARE NOT PERMITTED.

REQUEST FOR RESCHEDULING

☐ Please reschedule my appointment. Once USCIS receives your request, you will be sent a new appointment notice. Make a copy of this notice for your records, then mail the original with your request to BPU, Alexandria ASC, Suite 100, 8850 Richmond Hwy, Alexandria, VA 22309-1586

BIOMETRICS PROCESSING STAMP
ASC SITE CODE
BIOMETRICS QA REVIEW BY
9149672 ON
TENPRINTS QA REVIEW BY
9149672 ON   SEP 2 8 2014

APPLICATION NUMBER
I485 - SRC1423750478

If you have any questions regarding this notice, please call 1-800-375-5283.

WARNING: *Due to limited seating availability in our lobby area, only persons who are necessary to assist with transportation or completing the biometrics worksheet should accompany you. If you have open wounds or bandages/casts when you appear, the USCIS may reschedule your appointment if it is determined your injuries will interfere with taking your biometrics.*

44

Please see the back of this notice for important information.

TAB M
Respondent's Updated California Criminal History Information (CALDOJ)

May 10, 2016

RE: California Criminal History Information

Dear Applicant:

   This is in response to your record review request concerning the existence of a California criminal history record maintained in the files of the Department of Justice's Bureau of Criminal Information and Analysis. Your fingerprints did identify to an existing California criminal history record and a copy of that record is enclosed. If you wish to challenge the accuracy or completeness of your record, please complete and return the enclosed form (BCIA 8706) and supporting documentation to the address noted above.

   Pursuant to California Penal Code section 11121, the purpose of a record review request is to afford an individual with a copy of their record and to refute any erroneous or inaccurate information contained therein. The intent is not to be used for licensing, certification or employment purposes.

   Additionally, California Penal Code sections 11125, 11142, and 11143 does not allow for a person or agency to make a request to another person to provide them with a copy of an individual's criminal history or notification that a record does not exist; does not allow an authorized person to furnish the record to an unauthorized person; nor does it allow an unauthorized person to buy, receive or possess the record or information. A violation of these section codes is a misdemeanor.

                         Sincerely,

                         Cindy Santos

                         Record Review Unit
                         Applicant Information and Certification Program
                         Bureau of Criminal Information and Analysis

                    For KAMALA D. HARRIS
                         Attorney General

Enclosures
BCIA 8711 (Rev. 06/10)

46

```
4CMTDP298338.IH
RE: QHX.CA0349400.28402571(    )PUSR.    DATE:20160510 TIME:(   37:28
RESTRICTED-DO NOT USE FOR EMPLOYMENT,LICENSING OR CERTIFICATION PURPOSES
ATTN:APPUSR


*********************************************************************
FOR CALIFORNIA AGENCIES ONLY - HAS PREVIOUS QUALIFYING OFFENSE.  COLLECT
DNA IF INCARCERATED, CONFINED, OR ON PROBATION OR PAROLE FOLLOWING ANY
MISDEMEANOR OR FELONY CONVICTION.  REQUEST KITS AND INFO AT (510) 620-
3300 OR PC296.PC296@DOJ.CA.GOV.
*********************************************************************
** PALM PRINT ON FILE AT DOJ FOR ADDITIONAL INFORMATION PLEASE E-MAIL
PALM.PRINT@DOJ.CA.GOV
** III CALIFORNIA ONLY SOURCE RECORD
CII/A28402571
DOB/19790126    SEX/F RAC/HISPANIC
HGT/500  WGT/160  EYE/BRO  HAI/BRO  POB/PI
CTZ/PHILIPPINES
NAM/001
    002  ███████████████████

FBI/679551RC6
DMV/B7612926
SOC/607221783
SMT/TAT BACK-UNKNOWN            ; TAT L ANKL-UNKNOWN            ;
    TAT R SHLD-UNKNOWN
* * * *

ARR/DET/CITE:        NAM:001  DOB:19790126
20070602    CAPD FRESNO

CNT:001      #0766634-428787
   470(D) PC-FALSE CHECKS/RECORDS/CERTS/ETC        TOC:F
   SCN:S49A1530023
- - - -
COURT:              NAM:001
20070724  CASC FRESNO CENTRAL

CNT:001      #F107904397
   470(D) PC-FALSE CHECKS/RECORDS/CERTS/ETC        TOC:F
   DISPO:DISMISSED

CNT:002
   530.5(A) PC-GET CREDIT/ETC:USE OTHER'S ID        TOC:F
   DISPO:DISMISSED

CNT:003
   496(A) PC-RECEIVE/ETC KNOWN STOLEN PROPERTY        TOC:F
   DISPO:DISMISSED

CNT:004
   484E(D) PC-USE ACCESS ACCOUNT INFO W/O CONSENT    TOC:F
*DISPO:CONVICTED
   CONV STATUS:MISDEMEANOR
   SEN: 036 MONTHS PROBATION, 003 DAYS JAIL, 003 DAYS JAIL OR FINE,
        FINE, RESTN

DISPO:CONVICTION CERT BY CLERK OF THE COURT
DISPO:FOR CERT INFO SEE AUTOMATED ARCHIVE SYS

20081229
DISPO:EARLY DISMISSAL FROM PROBATION
* * * *
```

47

```
ARR/DET/CITE:          NAM:001  DOB:19790126
20080325    CAPD FRESNO

CNT:001     #0886809-428787
  11377(A) HS-POSSESS CONTROLLED SUBSTANCE          TOC:F

CNT:002
  11550(A) HS-USE/UNDER INFL CONTRLD SUBSTANCE      TOC:M
   SCN:S49B0850009
- - - -
COURT:              NAM:001
20080514  CASC FRESNO CENTRAL

CNT:001     #F08902017
  11550(A) HS-USE/UNDER INFL CONTRLD SUBSTANCE      TOC:M
 DISPO:DISMISSED

CNT:002
  11377(A) HS-POSSESS CONTROLLED SUBSTANCE          TOC:F
 DISPO:PROC SUSP/DRUG CRT-DEFERRED JUDGEMENT

20081229
 DISPO:DRG CRT/DEFER JDGMNT-TRM CRM PROC REINST
- - - -
COURT:              NAM:001
20081229  CASC FRESNO CENTRAL

CNT:001     #F08902017
  11377(A) HS-POSSESS CONTROLLED SUBSTANCE          TOC:F
*DISPO:CONVICTED
   CONV STATUS:FELONY
   SEN: 024 MONTHS PROBATION, 002 DAYS JAIL, WORK PROGRAM, IMP SEN SS

 DISPO:COND OF PROB-DRUG TREATMENT PLACEMENT
* * * *

ARR/DET/CITE:          NAM:001  DOB:19790126
20081201    CAPD FRESNO

CNT:001     #08103848-428787
  11377(A) HS-POSSESS CONTROLLED SUBSTANCE          TOC:F

CNT:002
  11364 HS-POSSESS CONTROL SUBSTANCE PARAPHERNA     TOC:M

CNT:003
  12316(B)(1) PC-PROHIBITED OWN/ETC AMMO/ETC        TOC:F
   ADR:20081201 (200,LOMA, ,S,LA,CA,90026)
   SCN:S49B3360019
- - - -
COURT:              NAM:001
20081229  CASC FRESNO CENTRAL

CNT:001     #F08907500
  11364 HS-POSSESS CONTROL SUBSTANCE PARAPHERNA     TOC:M
 DISPO:DISMISSED

CNT:002
  11377(A) HS-POSSESS CONTROLLED SUBSTANCE          TOC:F
*DISPO:CONVICTED
   CONV STATUS:FELONY
   SEN: 024 MONTHS PROBATION, 001 DAYS JAIL, WORK PROGRAM, IMP SEN SS

 DISPO:COND OF PROB-DRUG TREATMENT PLACEMENT
```

TAB N
Fresno County Sheriff's Department Arrest Report, California Superior Court Criminal Complaint and Plea Form (F07904397)

FRESNO COUNTY SHERIFF'S DEPARTMENT ARREST REPORT

R 07904397

Booking No:	JID:	Name(Last, First Middle):	Area: NW	Zone: 2048	Report Number: 07047548 - 1

Street Address: 310 G ST	City: FRESNO	Zip Code: 93721	Yrs / Mos:	Residence Phone:	Alias:

Race: A	Age: 28	Sex: F	Eye Color: BRO	Hair Color: BLK	Wgt: 100	Hgt: 500	DOB: 01/26/1979	Eth:	POB - City: PHILLAPINES	POB - State:

Scars/marks/tattoos:
TAT R SHD BUTTERFLY KISSING FLOWER / TAT L ANK FLOWER W/DESIGN / TAT BACK TINKER BELL

SSN:	Drvr.Lic.#: B7612926	St: CA	FBI No:	SID No:	CDC No:	

Arrival Date:	Arrival Time:	Arrest Date: 06/02/2007	Arrest Time: 21:55	Arrest Location: 3259 N DEWEY AV / W FEDORA AV

Arrest Agency: FPD	Arrest Officer: WALKER (V3273), KIM - P1222	Comp. #:

Transporting Officer: WALKER (V3273), KIM - P1222	Agency: PD	From: LOA	To: I BUREAU

Transporting Officer: -	Agency: PD	From: I BUREAU	To: FCJ

Blood Alcohol Level:	Condition: OK	Attitude: COOPERATIVE	Employer Name:	Occupation: NONE

Hair Length: SHLDR	Hair Style: STRAIGHT	Facial Hair:	Complexion: MEDIUM	Build: THIN	Clothing: JEANS, BROWN TANK TOP

Nearest Relative or Friend: NONE	Address:	Phone:

Injury/Illness: NONE STATED	Medical Attention:	

License:	State:	Year:	Make:	Model:	Color:	Released To:

Arrest Details:
SUBJECT WAS CONTACTED AT RESIDENCE AND FOUND TO HAVE SEVERAL ALTERED CHECKS IN HER POSSESSION.

The above offense(s) was/were committed in my presence and under the authority of California Penal Code section 837, I hereby arrest and deliver to the Fresno County Sheriff's Department for Transportation and Booking, the above listed suspect on the above listed charges. I have knowledge that knowingly making a false arrest is a criminal offense (Cal. P.C. 148.5).

_____
Signature of Arresting Citizen

Address

Phone

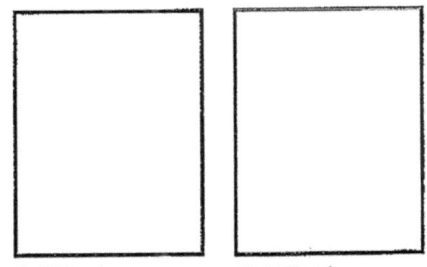

_____
Signature of Person Being Arrested

Left Thumb:

Right Thumb:

50

65

Page: 1 of 2

FRESNO COUNTY SHERIFF'S DEPARTMENT ARREST REPORT

Booking No:	JID:	Name(Last, First Middle):		Area: NW	Zone: 2048	Report Number: 07047548 - 1

Street Address: 310 G ST			City: FRESNO	Zip Code: 93721	Yrs / Mos:	Residence Phone:	Alias:

Race: A	Age: 28	Sex: F	Eye Color: BRO	Hair Color: BLK	Wgt: 100	Hgt: 500	DOB: 01/26/1979	Eth:	POB - City: PHILLAPINES	POB - State:

Charge: PC 470(D)	Counts: 1	Drug Weight/Amount:

Warrant No.:	Judicial District: FRESNO MUNI	Judge:	DOI:	Ball Amount[]

66

51

SUPERIOR COURT OF CALIFORNIA, COUNTY OF FRESNO

CENTRAL DIVISION

FILED

JUN 0 5 2007

FRESNO COUNTY SUPERIOR COURT

By_____ DEPUTY

THE PEOPLE OF THE STATE OF CALIFORNIA,	COMPLAINT - CRIMINAL
Plaintiff	FELONY COMPLAINT
vs.	COURT CASE NO. (07904397
▮▮▮▮▮▮▮▮▮▮	DA FILE NO. 2007F22182
Defendant(s)	O1F10 47,00

Agency: Fresno Police Department

Agency Report Number: 07-47548

Defendant

▮▮▮▮▮▮▮▮▮

Birth Date
01/26/1979

Booking No.
07-10171

Personally appeared before me, who first being duly sworn, complains and alleges:

COUNT 1

On or about June 2, 2007, in the above named judicial district, the crime of FORGERY, in violation of PENAL CODE SECTION 470(d), a felony, was committed by Anna Carissa Estaya Unlayao, who did, with the intent to defraud, falsely make, alter, forge and counterfeit, utter, publish, pass and attempt to offer to pass, as true and genuine, Checks, knowing the same to be false, altered, forged and counterfeited.

*****

COUNT 2

On or about June 2, 2007, in the above named judicial district, the crime of ACQUISITION OF ACCESS CARD ACCOUNT INFORMATION, in violation of PENAL CODE SECTION 484e(d), a felony, was committed by ▮▮▮▮▮▮▮▮▮▮ who acquired and retained possession of access card account information with respect to an access card validly issued to another person, without the cardholder's and issuer's consent, with intent to use it fraudulently.

*****

COUNT 3

On or about June 2, 2007, in the above named judicial district, the crime of IDENTITY THEFT, in violation of PENAL CODE SECTION 530.5(a), a felony, was committed by Anna Carissa Estaya Unlayao, who did willfully obtain personal identifying information on ▮▮▮▮▮▮▮▮ and unlawfully use that information to obtain, and attempt to obtain, credit, goods and services in the name of ▮▮▮▮▮▮▮ without consent.

*****

COUNT 4

On or about June 2, 2007, in the above named judicial district, the crime of RECEIVING STOLEN PROPERTY - PERSONAL PROPERTY, in violation of PENAL CODE SECTION 496(a), a felony, was committed by Anna Carissa Estaya Unlayao, who did unlawfully buy, receive, conceal, sell, withhold, or aid in concealing, selling, or withholding personal property belonging to ▮▮▮▮ ▮▮▮▮▮▮ which had been stolen, knowing that said property had been stolen.

*****

sv 6.5.07   Page 1

All of which is contrary to the form, force, and effect of the Statute in such case made and provided, and against the peace and dignity of the people of the State of California.

* * * * *

Pursuant to Penal Code Sections 1054.5(b), the People are hereby informally requesting that defense counsel provide discovery to the People as required by Penal Code Section 1054.3.

Pursuant to Penal Code Section 1054.2, no attorney may disclose or permit to be disclosed to a defendant, members of the defendant's family, or anyone else, the address or telephone number of a victim or witness whose name is disclosed pursuant to Penal Code Section 1054.1(a), unless ordered by the court. Willful violation of this section by an attorney, persons employed by an attorney, or persons appointed by the court is a misdemeanor.

The People of the State of California hereby give notice that the prosecution will allege and prove any and all applicable California Rules of Court, Rule 4.421 facts in aggravation pursuant to *Blakely v. Washington,* 542 U.S. 296 (2004) and *Cunningham v. California,* 542 U.S. ___ [2007 WL 135687]. The People of the State of California will allege said aggravating factors in the Information and hereby further reserve the right to present any and all applicable aggravating facts conforming to proof at trial.

Subscribed and sworn to before me on

DATE: ___6|5|0 ___

Attest:

_____
DEPUTY CLERK

_____
COMPLAINANT

53

SUPERIOR COURT OF CALIFORNIA • COUNTY OF FRESNO
1100 Van Ness Avenue
Fresno, California 93724-0002

PLAINTIFF: PEOPLE OF THE STATE OF CALIFORNIA

DEFENDANT: ███████████

MISDEMEANOR
ADVISEMENT, WAIVER OF RIGHTS, AND PLEA FORM

CASE NUMBER:
F 07 9 0 4 3 9 7

I understand the **nature of the charges** against me and I request to withdraw my plea(s) of not guilty and now plead ☐ GUILTY ☒ NO CONTEST to the following violation(s) of law (list counts, code sections, priors, and any conditions of the plea):

PC 984 e(d)

RIGHT TO AN ATTORNEY:
I understand I have the right to be represented by an attorney at all stages of the proceedings, and if I am unable to afford an attorney, the court will appoint one for me.

1. I have had enough time to discuss my case and all possible defenses with my attorney . . . .

2. I GIVE UP MY RIGHT to have an attorney represent me. . . . .

CONSTITUTIONAL RIGHTS:
I understand I am presumed innocent and the State is required to prove me guilty beyond a reasonable doubt. I also understand that I have the following constitutional rights as to all matters charged against me:

	I understand this right	I give up this right
1. The right to a speedy, public JURY or COURT TRIAL.		
2. The right to be CONFRONTED by WITNESSES against me; that is, to see, hear and question all witnesses against me.		
3. The right to NOT INCRIMINATE MYSELF; that is, not to be compelled to testify against myself though I may testify if I choose to do so. . . . . :		
4. The right to PRESENT EVIDENCE at no cost to me and to have the court issue subpenas to bring into court all witnesses and evidence favorable to me.		

CONSEQUENCES OF PLEA OF GUILTY OR NO CONTEST: I understand:

1. If I am presently on parole or probation, my change of plea could be a reason for finding me in violation of my parole or probation. . . . .

2. If I am not a citizen, my change of plea can result in my deportation, exclusion from admission to the United States, and/or a denial of naturalization. Deportation may be mandatory for this offense. I have fully discussed this my attorney and understand the serious immigration consequences of my plea. . . . .

3. The maximum sentence I can receive as a result of my plea   1 yr + $2,000

4. Other possible consequences of this plea will include a restitution fine of $100 to $1000, and may include (e.g. registration): _____

5. The facts on which I base my plea are: _____ people v. ███████ _____ | [initials]

6. I am entering my plea freely and voluntarily without fear or threat to me or anyone closely related to me. . . . . | [initials]

7. The matter of probation and sentence is to be determined solely by the Court. . . . . | [initials]

8. I understand that I have the right to wait a minimum of six hours, and up to five days to be sentenced. I give up this right and agree to be sentenced at this time. . . . . | [initials]

9. I understand that I may be required to provide buccal swab samples and any blood specimens or other biological samples required for law enforcement identification analysis. | [X]

I declare under PENALTY OF PERJURY, under the laws of the State of California, that I have read, understood, and initialed each item above, and everything on this form is true and correct.

Date: _____ 7-24-07 _____   Signed: X _____ [signature] _____
                                                    (Defendant)

WAIVER OF PRESENCE/JUDGE

I hereby waive my right to be present and I authorize my attorney to enter the plea on my behalf. I agree to be sentenced at the time the plea is entered. I authorize my attorney to accept the court's orders and conditions on my behalf, if any, imposed on me.

I understand that I have the right to enter my plea before and be sentenced by a judge. I give up this right and agree to be sentenced by a temporary judge.

Date: _____   Signed: _____
                                              (Defendant)

ATTORNEY'S STATEMENT

I am the attorney of record for the defendant and have reviewed this form with my client. I have explained to the defendant of his/her rights and answered all of the defendant's questions with regard to this plea. I have discussed the facts the case with the defendant, and explained the consequences of this plea, the elements of the offense(s), and the possible defense(s). I concur with this plea and the defendant's decision to waive his/her constitutional rights.

Date: _____ 7-24-07 _____   Signed: _____ [signature] _____
                                                    (Attorney for Defendant)

INTERPRETER'S STATEMENT (IF APPLICABLE)

I, _____, have been duly sworn and have truly translated this form to the defendant in the _____ language. The defendant indicated that (s)he understood the contents of the form, and (s)he has initialed the form.

Date: _____   Signed: _____
                                              (Court Interpreter)

COURT'S FINDINGS AND ORDER

The Court, having reviewed this form and having questioned the defendant concerning the defendant's constitutional rights, accepts the defendant's plea(s) and the factual basis for the plea(s), and finds that the defendant has expressly, knowingly, understandingly, and intelligently waived his/her constitutional rights. The Court finds that the defendant's plea(s) is freely and voluntarily made with an understanding of the nature and consequences of the plea(s). The defendant is convicted on the basis of his/her plea(s).

The Court orders this form filed and entered in this case.

Date: _____ 7-24-07 _____   Signed: _____ [signature] _____
                                                    (Judge of Superior Court)

FCR-42 R06-05

MISDEMEANOR
ADVI___ ENT, WAIVER OF RIGHTS, AND PLEA FC___

55

TAB O
Letter from Respondent's Mother

May 20, 2016

Dear Immigration Judge,

My name is ████████████████████████████ I came to America in 1983. My siblings and I acquired our US citizenship as a derivatives of our father Santiago Estaya Sr. When we growing up in the Philippines we know that we are All American citizens. My father said because he was naturalized after the war in 1949 and granted the US citizenship in Batangas, Philippines. We often ask our father how did it happened, how he was granted the US citizenship, before he even came to America. He just answered with a smile. I always thought he was simply really a good man who love his family and his country. He was proud to be an American and so do us, his children. Some three years ago, out of curiosity I google my father's name, and to my amazement I found his name listed on the book titled "The Hour of Redemptions". This is about the Last raid in Cabanatuan, an effort to rescue more than 500 US soldiers POW'S. He was one of the Philippines Scout who helped the US Armed Forces. Now, I know why he was granted the US citizenship before he even step his feet on American soil. He was awarded the "Bronze Star for Heroic Achievement on January 30, 1945, along with it is also his US Naturalization. I am so very proud that I am his daughter.

My daughter, ████████████ is my father's youngest granddaughter when he passed away in December of 1982, if he is alive now it will break his heart to pieces to see his granddaughter to be deported. My daughter's family is here in United States. Her daughter ███is here, it will be devastated to break them apart. Mila is her life. We don't want Mila to grow up without a mother. My husband and I and her siblings and her niece ███are all here. Her bond with my other daughter ███ is exceptional they love each other so much. They always talked about the future of their kids growing up and raising them together.

Yes, she may have done some crazy things before, but she is change woman now. She worked hard as a caregiver and she is an excellent one. She went to school to become a drug counselor, but job is so scarce nowadays. And she love taking care of old folks, possibly reminding her of grandma and grandpa.

57

When I had my children in the Philippines, I thought my children are all citizen of the United States and will have the same status like myself. I was a very young mother, I had my 3 children before I marry their father. My mother last wished to me is not to marry right away because we were young and there is no divorce in the Philippines. So we decided not get married until October of 1984. When I went to US embassy in Manila they told me that I have to file a petition for them. During the years, I was working so, hard to make ends meet and I forgot to file a citizenship papers for them and because of my neglect Anna Carissa's s is subject to deportation. Please my heartfelt plea, Your Honor, please don't separate our family again. Anna Carissa and her daughter need to be here at the same place. Anna Carissa deserve another chance and let us be happy as one family and hopefully she will get her citizenship because I was unable to report and register them at the US Immigration in Manila after their birth, due to my innocence or lack of knowledge at that time. When eldest son Edmund and Anna Carissa they received their original Green Card it has no expiration date. I was robbed at a shopping Mall in the 1990's, and I have her original green card in my purse along with my other papers. So when I received a new one, I have my husband to hide it so it will not get lost again. Didn't realize until later on when she went to the cruise that there is an expiration date, who would have thought. And that is the reason why she is in this position right now.

Your Honor, please do not deport our daughter, this is the only home that she has ever known ever since she came here in 1990. It will be a great lost for her and her daughter to be separated from each and the family that loves her.

Respectfully,

███████████

TAB P
Letter of Employment

AROUND THE CLOCK
INTEGRITY ~ TRUST ~ COMPASSION ~ HEALING
Partners In Care

HOME CARE
Home Health Services

COMPANION CARE
Personal Care Services
Bakersfield
Fresno

REPRESENTATIVE/PAYEE
Representative Payee Program

CAREGIVER TRAINING & ASSISTANCE
Training/Support Programs

5/9/16

To Whom it May Concern,

This letter is to speak of the character of ▮▮▮▮▮▮▮▮▮▮▮▮▮▮▮ has worked for me at Around the Clock Companion Care since December 29th, 2015. I am the person responsible for hiring her and managing her as well as my other employees on a daily basis. Since she begun working for me, she has been very responsible, caring and dependable. Our elderly clients love her and our client's children feel very safe knowing that their parents are in good hands. With her current work ethic and motivated state of mind, I feel very confident that he will work for us for many years to come. I hope this letter helps speak of her tremendous character.

Thank you,

Brandon Miller
Staffing Supervisor
Around the Clock Care

(559) 320-2400
bmiller@bakersfieldcare.com

Over 25 Years of Service to Kern County
Est. 1985

5251 Office Park Drive, Suite 400
Bakersfield, CA 93309
phone 661-395-5800
fax 661-864-0732
bakersfieldcare.com

60

TAB Q
Additional Letters of Support

California Association of Addiction Recovery Resources
P.O. Box 214127, Sacramento, CA 95821
916-338-9460 ~ FAX: 916-338-9468
TTY: 916-473-0836

<u>**KEEP THIS LETTER FOR YOUR RECORDS AND YOUR EMPLOYER!**</u>

January 19, 2012

███████████████████████

Dear ███████

This letter confirms your CAS registration #11836. The State of California, Department of Alcohol and Drug Programs, Counselor Certification Regulations requires that you complete the certification process within FIVE years from the date of registration. Your date of registration is: 1/19/2012. You are current through: 12/31/2012.

Your registration will need to be renewed annually until you become certified. Every year you are required to have three hours total of ethics and confidentiality trainings.

Good luck with your certification process, and please contact us with any further questions or concerns.

Sincerely,

Ken Jones
Operations Director

www.caarr.org

ICDC COLLEGE®

MAIN CAMPUS
6812 PACIFIC BLVD
HUNTINGTON PARK CA 90255
TEL 323 277 0240 / FAX 323 277

CORPORATE HEADQUARTERS
11859 WILSHIRE BLVD STE 600
LOS ANGELES CA 90025
TEL. 310 482 6996 / FAX 310 473 2048

CORPORATE / ONLINE OFFICE
5995 SEPULVEDA BLVD
CULVER CITY CA 90230
TEL 310 482 6996 / FAX 310 482

December 2, 2015

Immigration Judge
U. S. Department of Homeland Security
606 S Olive St Floor 16
Court Room 1
Los Angeles CA 90014-1660

Re: Character Reference for ███████████

The Honorable Immigration Judge,

I have known ███████████, since January 18, 2011. She graduated from the ICDC College 9-month Alcohol & Drug Counseling vocation program, and successfully completed her externship on November 2, 2011. Anna Unlayao was a good student, actively participated in group counseling sessions, learned the 12 core functions, and developed her documentation skills.

I can confirm that ████ is a person of compassion and integrity. She is dedicated to her field of study and seeking gainful employment as a Substance Abuse Counselor.

Sincerely,

Victor Martinez

Victor Martinez
Career Advisor
ICDC College
6812 Pacific Blvd
Huntington Park CA 90255
(323) 277 0240 x325

63

DIPLOMA

PRESENTED TO

Has successfully completed a training course

Alcohol and Drug Counseling

at

ICDC COLLEGE

5422 Sunset Blvd.,
Hollywood, CA 90027

Revekka Gleykher,
Executive Director

11/02/11
Date

Marijna Frid,
Campus President, Hollywood Campus

11/02/11
Date

G4

To Whom It May Concern:

My name is Cindy Streufert. I was born in Wantagh, N.Y and moved to Fresno Ca in 1980. I have lived in the United States all my life (56 years) and am a proud, legal citizen of the United States.

I've worked at Boler, Fransen, Sawyers LLP for 18 years. I've known Carissa for at least 15 of those years. She dated my oldest son for quite some time.

In all the years I have known Carissa she has been happy, polite, a hard worker & an extremely faithful young woman. I have also come to know her as a wonderful mother & friend – Sincerely,

Cindy Streufert

TAB R
Respondent's 2015 Income Tax Return

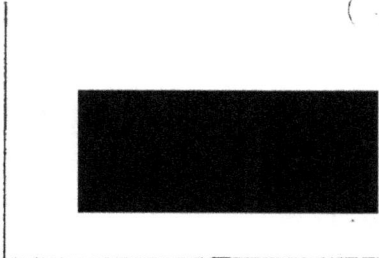

| | | | | Spouse's social security no. |

⚠ Make sure the SSN(s) above and on line 6c are correct.

Presidential Election Campaign
Check here if you, or your spouse if filing jointly, want $3 to go to this fund. Checking a box below will not change your tax or refund. ☐ You ☐ Spouse

Filing status
Check only one box.

1 ☒ Single
2 ☐ Married filing jointly (even if only one had income)
3 ☐ Married filing separately. Enter spouse's SSN above and full name here. ▶
4 ☐ Head of household (with qualifying person). (See instructions.) If the qualifying person is a child but not your dependent, enter this child's name here. ▶
5 ☐ Qualifying widow(er) with dependent child (see instructions)

Exemptions

6a ☒ **Yourself.** If someone can claim you as a dependent, **do not** check box 6a.

b ☐ Spouse

c Dependents:		(2) Dependent's social security number	(3) Dependent's relationship to you	(4) ✓ if child under age 17 qualifying for child tax cr. (see inst.)
(1) First name	Last name			
▆▆▆▆▆▆▆▆	▆▆▆▆▆	▆▆▆-▆▆-▆▆▆▆	DAUGHTER	☒

If more than six dependents, see inst.

Boxes checked on 6a and 6b ▶ **1**

No. of children on 6c who:
● lived with you **1**
● did not live with you due to divorce or separation (see inst.)
Dependents on 6c not entered above

d Total number of exemptions claimed.

Add numbers on lines above ▶ **2**

Income

Attach Form(s) W-2 here. Also attach Form(s) 1099-R if tax was withheld.

If you did not get a W-2, see instructions.

7	Wages, salaries, tips, etc. Attach Form(s) W-2.	7	4,011
8a	**Taxable interest.** Attach Schedule B if required.	8a	
b	**Tax-exempt interest. Do not** include on line 8a. 8b		
9a	Ordinary dividends. Attach Schedule B if required.	9a	
b	Qualified dividends (see instructions). 9b		
10	Capital gain distributions (see instructions).	10	
11a	IRA distributions. 11a	11b Taxable amount (see instructions).	11b	
12a	Pensions and annuities. 12a	12b Taxable amount (see instructions).	12b	
13	Unemployment compensation and Alaska Permanent Fund dividends.	13	1,365
14a	Social security benefits. 14a	14b Taxable amount (see instructions).	14b	
15	Add lines 7 through 14b (far right column). This is your **total income.** ▶	15	5,376

Adjusted gross income

16	Educator expenses (see instructions). 16		
17	IRA deduction (see instructions). 17		
18	Student loan interest deduction (see instructions). 18		
19	Tuition and fees. Attach Form 8917. 19		
20	Add lines 16 through 19. These are your **total adjustments.**	20	
21	Subtract line 20 from line 15. This is your **adjusted gross income.** ▶	21	5,376

For Disclosure, Privacy Act, and Paperwork Reduction Act Notice, see separate instructions.

Form **1040A** (2015)

FDA 15 1040A1 BWF 1040 Form Software Copyright 1996 – 2016 HRB Tax Group, Inc.

67

Tax, credits, and payments	22	Enter the amount from line 21 (adjusted gross income).	22	5,376
	23a	Check if: You were born before Jan. 2, 1951, ☐ Blind ☐ Spouse was born before Jan. 2, 1951, ☐ Blind ☐ Total boxes checked ▶ 23a		
Standard Deduction for—	b	If you are married filing separately and your spouse itemizes deductions, check here ▶ 23b ☐		
● People who check any box on line 23a or 23b or who can be claimed as a dependent, see instructions.	24	Enter your **standard deduction.**	24	6,300
	25	Subtract line 24 from line 22. If line 24 is more than line 22, enter -0-.	25	0
	26	**Exemptions.** Multiply $4,000 by the number on line 6d.	26	8,000
	27	Subtract line 26 from line 25. If line 26 is more than line 25, enter -0-. This is your **taxable income.** ▶ 27		0
● All others: Single or Married filing separately, $6,300	28	**Tax,** including any alternative minimum tax (see inst.) 28		0
	29	Excess advance premium tax credit repayment. Attach Form 8962. 29		
Married filing jointly or Qualifying widow(er), $12,600	30	Add lines 28 and 29.	30	
	31	Credit for child and dependent care expenses. Attach Form 2441. 31		
	32	Credit for the elderly or the disabled. Attach Schedule R. 32		
	33	Education credits from Form 8863, line 19. 33		
Head of household, $9,250	34	Retirement savings contributions credit. Attach Form 8880. 34		
	35	Child tax credit. Attach Schedule 8812, if required. 35		
	36	Add lines 31 through 35. These are your **total credits.**	36	0
	37	Subtract line 36 from line 30. If line 36 is more than line 30, enter -0-.	37	0
	38	Health care: individual responsibility (see instructions). Full-year coverage ☒	38	
	39	Add line 37 and line 38. This is your **total tax.**	39	0
	40	Federal income tax withheld from Forms W-2 and 1099. 40		68
If you have a qualifying child, attach Schedule EIC.	41	2015 estimated tax payments and amount applied from 2014 return. 41		
	42a	**Earned income credit (EIC).** 42a		1,369
	b	Nontaxable combat pay election. 42b		
	43	Additional child tax credit. Attach Schedule 8812. 43		152
	44	American opportunity credit from Form 8863, line 8. 44		
	45	Net premium tax credit. Attach Form 8962. 45		
	46	Add lines 40, 41, 42a, 43, 44, and 45. These are your **total payments.** ▶ 46		1,589
	47	If line 46 is more than line 39, subtract line 39 from line 46. This is the amount you **overpaid.**	47	1,589
Refund	48a	Amount of line 47 you want **refunded to you.** If Form 8888 is attached, check here ▶ ☐	48a	1,589
Direct deposit? See instructions and fill in 48b, 48c, and 48d or Form 8888.	▶b	Routing number	▶ c Type: ☒ Checking ☐ Savings	
	▶d	Account number		
	49	Amount of line 47 you want **applied to your 2016 estimated tax.** 49		
Amount you owe	50	**Amount you owe.** Subtract line 46 from line 39. For details on how to pay, see instructions. ▶ 50		
	51	Estimated tax penalty (see instructions). 51		

CLIENT COPY

Third party designee

Do you want to allow another person to discuss this return with the IRS (see instructions)? ☒ **Yes.** Complete the following. ☐ No

Designee's name ▶ HRB TAX GROUP INC   Phone no. ▶ 559-324-8491   Personal identification number (PIN) ▶ 06374

Sign here

Under penalties of perjury, I declare that I have examined this return and accompanying schedules and statements, and to the best of my knowledge and belief, they are true, correct, and accurately list all amounts and sources of income I received during the tax year. Declaration of preparer (other than the taxpayer) is based on all information of which the preparer has any knowledge.

Joint return? See instructions. Keep a copy for your records.

Your signature	Date	Your occupation CARE GIVER	Daytime phone number
Spouse's signature. If a joint rtn., **both** must sign.	Date	Spouse's occupation	If the IRS sent you an Identity Protection PIN, enter it here (see inst.)

Paid preparer use only

Print/type preparer's name RENUKA JAYAKRISHNAN	Preparer's signature	Date 02-09-2016	Check ☐ if self-employed	PTIN P01277350
Firm's name ▶ HRB TAX GROUP INC			Firm's EIN ▶ 431871840	
Firm's address ▶ 1610 HERNDON AVE CLOVIS CA 93611		Phone no. 5593248491		

SCHEDULE EIC
(Form 1040A or 1040)

Department of the Treasury
Internal Revenue Service (99)

Earned Income Credit
Qualifying Child Information

▶ **Complete and attach to Form 1040A or 1040 only if you have a qualifying child.**
▶ **Information about Schedule EIC (Form 1040A or 1040) and its instructions is at www.irs.gov/scheduleeic.**

1040A
1040
EIC

OMB No. 1545-0074

2015

Attachment
Sequence No. **43**

Name(s) shown on return

Your social security number

Before you begin:

- See the instructions for Form 1040A, lines 42a and 42b, or Form 1040, lines 66a and 66b, to make sure that **(a)** you can take the EIC, and **(b)** you have a qualifying child.
- Be sure the child's name on line 1 and social security number (SSN) on line 2 agree with the child's social security card. Otherwise, at the time we process your return, we may reduce or disallow your EIC. If the name or SSN on the child's social security card is not correct, call the Social Security Administration at 1-800-772-1213.

! CAUTION

- You can't claim the EIC for a child who didn't live with you for more than half of the year.
- If you take the EIC even though you are not eligible, you may not be allowed to take the credit for up to 10 years. See the instructions for details.
- It will take us longer to process your return and issue your refund if you do not fill in all lines that apply for each qualifying child.

Qualifying Child Information	Child 1		Child 2		Child 3	
1 Child's name If you have more than three qualifying children, you have to list only three to get the maximum credit.	First name	Last name	First name	Last name	First name	Last name
2 Child's SSN The child must have an SSN as defined in the instructions for Form 1040A, lines 42a and 42b, or Form 1040, lines 66a and 66b, unless the child was born and died in 2015. If your child was born and died in 2015 and did not have an SSN, enter "Died" on this line and attach a copy of the child's birth certificate, death certificate, or hospital medical records.	CLIENT COPY					
3 Child's year of birth	Year _2015_ If born after 1996 **and** the child is younger than you (or your spouse, if filing jointly), skip lines 4a and 4b; go to line 5.		Year _____ If born after 1996 **and** the child is younger than you (or your spouse, if filing jointly), skip lines 4a and 4b; go to line 5.		Year _____ If born after 1996 **and** the child is younger than you (or your spouse, if filing jointly), skip lines 4a and 4b; go to line 5.	
4a Was the child under age 24 at the end of 2015, a student, and younger than you (or your spouse, if filing jointly)?	☐ Yes. Go to line 5.	☐ No. Go to line 4b.	☐ Yes. Go to line 5.	☐ No. Go to line 4b.	☐ Yes. Go to line 5.	☐ No. Go to line 4b.
b Was the child permanently and totally disabled during any part of 2015?	☐ Yes. Go to line 5.	☐ No. The child is not a qualifying child.	☐ Yes. Go to line 5.	☐ No. The child is not a qualifying child.	☐ Yes. Go to line 5.	☐ No. The child is not a qualifying child.
5 Child's relationship to you (for example, son, daughter, grandchild, niece, nephew, foster child, etc.)	DAUGHTER					
6 Number of months child lived with you in the United States during 2015 • If the child lived with you for more than half of 2015 but less than 7 months, enter "7." • If the child was born or died in 2015 and your home was the child's home for more than half the time he or she was alive during 2015, enter "12."	_12_ months Do not enter more than 12 months.		_____ months Do not enter more than 12 months.		_____ months Do not enter more than 12 months.	

For Paperwork Reduction Act Notice, see your tax return instructions.

Schedule EIC (Form 1040A or 1040) 2015

FDA   **15 EIC1**   BWF 1040   Form Software Copyright 1996 – 2016 HRB Tax Group, Inc.

69

Child Tax Credit

▶ Attach to Form 1040, Form 1040A, or Form 1040NR.
▶ Information about Schedule 8812 and its separate instructions is at
www.irs.gov/schedule8812.

1040A
1040NR
8812

OMB No. 1545-0074

2015

Attachment
Sequence No. 47

Name(s) shown on return

Your social security number

Part I — Filers Who Have Certain Child Dependent(s) with an ITIN (Individual Taxpayer Identification Number)

CAUTION
Complete this part only for each dependent who has an ITIN and for whom you are claiming the child tax credit.
If your dependent is not a qualifying child for the credit, you cannot include that dependent in the calculation of this credit.

Answer the following questions for each dependent listed on Form 1040, line 6c; Form 1040A, line 6c; or Form 1040NR, line 7c, who has an ITIN (Individual Taxpayer Identification Number) and that you indicated is a qualifying child for the child tax credit by checking column (4) for that dependent.

A For the first dependent identified with an ITIN and listed as a qualifying child for the child tax credit, did this child meet the substantial presence test? See separate instructions.
☐ Yes   ☐ No

B For the second dependent identified with an ITIN and listed as a qualifying child for the child tax credit, did this child meet the substantial presence test? See separate instructions.
☐ Yes   ☐ No

C For the third dependent identified with an ITIN and listed as a qualifying child for the child tax credit, did this child meet the substantial presence test? See separate instructions.
☐ Yes   ☐ No

D For the fourth dependent identified with an ITIN and listed as a qualifying child for the child tax credit, did this child meet the substantial presence test? See separate instructions.
☐ Yes   ☐ No

CLIENT COPY

Note: If you have more than four dependents identified with an ITIN and listed as a qualifying child for the child tax credit, see separate instructions and check here ··· ▶ ☐

Part II — Additional Child Tax Credit Filers

1 If you file Form 2555 or 2555-EZ **stop here**, you cannot claim the additional child tax credit.
If you are required to use the worksheet in Pub. 972, enter the amount from line 8 of the Child Tax Credit Worksheet in the publication. Otherwise:

    1040 filers: Enter the amount from line 6 of your Child Tax Credit Worksheet (see the Instructions for Form 1040, line 52).

    1040A filers: Enter the amount from line 6 of your Child Tax Credit Worksheet (see the Instructions for Form 1040A, line 35).

    1040NR filers: Enter the amount from line 6 of your Child Tax Credit Worksheet (see the Instructions for Form 1040NR, line 49).

1		1,000

2 Enter the amount from Form 1040, line 52; Form 1040A, line 35; or Form 1040NR, line 49 ··············· **2** 0

3 Subtract line 2 from line 1. If zero, **stop**; you cannot take this credit ··························· **3** 1,000

4a Earned income (see separate instructions) ···························· **4a** 4,011

  b Nontaxable combat pay (see separate instr.) ··· **4b**

5 Is the amount on line 4a more than $3,000?
    ☐ **No.** Leave line 5 blank and enter –0– on line 6.
    ☒ **Yes.** Subtract $3,000 from the amount on line 4a. Enter the result ······· **5** 1,011

6 Multiply the amount on line 5 by 15% (.15) and enter the result ····························· **6** 152

  Next. Do you have three or more qualifying children?
    ☒ **No.** If line 6 is zero, stop; you cannot take this credit. Otherwise, skip Part III and enter the **smaller of** line 3 or line 6 on line 13.
    ☐ **Yes.** If line 6 is equal to or more than line 3, skip Part III and enter the amount from line 3 on line 13. Otherwise, go to line 7.

For Paperwork Reduction Act Notice, see your tax return instructions.

Schedule 8812 (Form 1040A or 1040) 2015

Part III	Certain Filers Who Have Three or More Qualifying Children		
7	Withheld social security, Medicare, and Additional Medicare taxes from Form(s) W-2, boxes 4 and 6. If married filing jointly, include your spouse's amounts with yours. If your employer withheld or you paid Additional Medicare Tax or tier 1 RRTA taxes, see separate instructions · · · · · · · · · · · · · · ·	**7**	
8	1040 filers: Enter the total of the amounts from Form 1040, lines 27 and 58, plus any taxes that you identified using code "UT" and entered on line 62. 1040A filers: Enter -0-. 1040NR filers: Enter the total of the amounts from Form 1040NR, lines 27 and 56, plus any taxes that you identified using code "UT" and entered on line 60.	**8**	
9	Add lines 7 and 8 ·	**9**	
10	1040 filers: Enter the total of the amounts from Form 1040, lines 66a and 71. 1040A filers: Enter the total of the amount from Form 1040A, line 42a, plus any excess social security and tier 1 RRTA taxes withheld that you entered to the left of line 46 (see separate instructions). 1040NR filers: Enter the amount from Form 1040NR, line 67.	**10**	
11	Subtract line 10 from line 9. If zero or less, enter -0- ·	**11**	
12	Enter the **larger** of line 6 or line 11 ·	**12**	
	Next, enter the **smaller** of line 3 or line 12 on line 13.		

Part IV	Additional Child Tax Credit		
13	This is your additional child tax credit ·	**13**	152

1040
1040A
1040NR

Enter this amount on
Form 1040, line 67,
Form 1040A, line 43, or
Form 1040NR, line 64.

CLIENT COPY

FDA   15 88122   BWF 1040   Form Software Copyright 1998 – 2016 HRB Tax Group, Inc.   Schedule 8812 (Form 1040A or 1040) 2015

71

Form 8867

Department of the Treasury
Internal Revenue Service

Paid Preparer's Earned Income Credit Checklist

▶ To be completed by preparer and filed with Form 1040, 1040A, or 1040EZ.
▶ Information about Form 8867 and its separate instructions is at www.irs.gov/form8867.

OMB No. 1545-1629

2015

Attachment
Sequence No. 177

Taxpayer name(s) shown on return

Taxpayer's social security number
607-22-1783

For the definitions of **Qualifying Child** and **Earned Income**, see Pub. 596.

Part I	All Taxpayers

1 Enter preparer's name and PTIN ▶ <u>RENUKA JAYAKRISHNAN P01277350</u>

2 Is the taxpayer's filing status married filing separately? . . . . ☐ Yes ☒ No

    ▶ If you checked **"Yes"** on line 2, **stop;** the taxpayer **cannot** take the EIC. Otherwise; continue.

3 Does the taxpayer (and the taxpayer's spouse if filing jointly) have a social security number (SSN) that allows him or her to work and is valid for EIC purposes? See the instructions before answering . . . . ☒ Yes ☐ No

    ▶ If you checked **"No"** on line 3, **stop;** the taxpayer **cannot** take the EIC. Otherwise, continue.

4 Is the taxpayer (or the taxpayer's spouse if filing jointly) filing Form 2555 or Form 2555-EZ (relating to the exclusion of foreign earned income)? . . . . ☐ Yes ☒ No

    ▶ If you checked **"Yes"** on line 4, **stop;** the taxpayer **cannot** take the EIC. Otherwise, continue.

5a Was the taxpayer (or the taxpayer's spouse) a nonresident alien for any part of 2015? . . . . ☐ Yes ☒ No

    ▶ If you checked **"Yes"** on line 5a, go to line 5b. Otherwise, skip line 5b and go to line 6.

b Is the taxpayer's filing status married filing jointly? . . . . CLIENT COPY . . . . . . ☐ Yes ☐ No

    ▶ If you checked **"Yes"** on line 5a and **"No"** on line 5b, **stop;** the taxpayer **cannot** take the EIC. Otherwise, continue.

6 Is the taxpayer's **investment income** more than $3,400? See the instructions before answering. . . . . ☐ Yes ☒ No

    ▶ If you checked **"Yes"** on line 6, **stop;** the taxpayer **cannot** take the EIC. Otherwise, continue.

7 Could the taxpayer be a **qualifying child** of another person for 2015? If the taxpayer's filing status is married filing jointly, check **"No."** Otherwise, see instructions before answering . . . . ☐ Yes ☒ No

    ▶ If you checked **"Yes"** on line 7, **stop;** the taxpayer **cannot** take the EIC. Otherwise, go to Part II or Part III, whichever applies.

For Paperwork Reduction Act Notice, see separate instructions.

Form **8867** (2015)

FDA 15 88671 BWF 1040 Form Software Copyright 1996 – 2016 HRB Tax Group, Inc.

72

Part II   Taxpayers With a Child

	Child 1	Child 2	Child 3
Caution. If there is more than one child, complete lines 8 through 14 for one child before going to the next column.			
8 Child's name	[redacted]		
9 Is the child the taxpayer's son, daughter, stepchild, foster child, brother, sister, stepbrother, stepsister, half brother, half sister, or a descendant of any of them?	☒ Yes ☐ No	☐ Yes ☐ No	☐ Yes ☐ No
10 Was the child unmarried at the end of 2015? If the child was married at the end of 2015, see the instructions before answering	☒ Yes ☐ No	☐ Yes ☐ No	☐ Yes ☐ No
11 Did the child live with the taxpayer in the United States for over half of 2015? See the instructions before answering ·	☒ Yes ☐ No	☐ Yes ☐ No	☐ Yes ☐ No
12 Was the child (at the end of 2015)— ● Under age 19 and younger than the taxpayer (or the taxpayer's spouse, if the taxpayer files jointly), ● Under age 24, a student (defined in the instructions), and younger than the taxpayer (or the taxpayer's spouse, if the taxpayer files jointly), or ● Any age and permanently and totally disabled? · · · · · · · · · · · · · · · · ·	☒ Yes ☐ No	☐ Yes ☐ No	☐ Yes ☐ No

▶ If you checked **"Yes"** on lines 9, 10, 11, **and** 12, the child is the taxpayer's qualifying child; go to line 13a. If you checked **"No"** on line 9, 10, 11, **or** 12, the child is not the taxpayer's qualifying child; see the instructions for line 12.

	Child 1	Child 2	Child 3
13a Do you or the taxpayer know of another person who could check **"Yes"** on lines 9, 10, 11, **and** 12 for the child? (If the only other person is the taxpayer's spouse, see the instructions before answering.) . . . . · · ·	☐ Yes ☒ No	☐ Yes ☐ No	☐ Yes ☐ No

▶ If you checked **"No"** on line 13a, go to line 14. Otherwise, go to line 13b.

b Enter the child's relationship to the other person(s) · · · · · · · · · · · · · · · · · · ·

	Child 1	Child 2	Child 3
c Under the tiebreaker rules, is the child treated as the taxpayer's qualifying child? See the instructions before answering	☐ Yes ☐ No ☐ Don't know	☐ Yes ☐ No ☐ Don't know	☐ Yes ☐ No ☐ Don't know

▶ If you checked **"Yes"** on line 13c, go to line 14. If you checked **"No,"** the taxpayer **cannot** take the EIC based on this child and cannot take the EIC for taxpayers who do not have a qualifying child. If there is more than one child, see the **Note** at the bottom of this page. If you checked **"Don't know,"** explain to the taxpayer that, under the tiebreaker rules, the taxpayer's EIC and other tax benefits may be disallowed. Then, if the taxpayer wants to take the EIC based on this child, complete lines 14 and 15. If not, and there are no other qualifying children, the taxpayer cannot take the EIC, including the EIC for taxpayers without a qualifying child; do not complete Part III. If there is more than one child, see the **Note** at the bottom of this page.

	Child 1	Child 2	Child 3
14 Does the qualifying child have an SSN that allows him or her to work and is valid for EIC purposes? See the instructions before answering · · · · · · · · · · · · · · ·	☒ Yes ☐ No	☐ Yes ☐ No	☐ Yes ☐ No

▶ If you checked **"No"** on line 14, the taxpayer **cannot** take the EIC based on this child and cannot take the EIC available to taxpayers without a qualifying child. If there is more than one child, see the **Note** at the bottom of this page. If you checked **"Yes"** on line 14, continue.

15 Are the taxpayer's **earned income** and **adjusted gross income** each less than the limit that applies to the taxpayer for 2015? See instructions . . . .   ☒ Yes ☐ No

▶ If you checked **"No"** on line 15, **stop**; the taxpayer **cannot** take the EIC. If you checked **"Yes"** on line 15, the taxpayer can take the EIC. Complete **Schedule EIC** and attach it to the taxpayer's return. If there are two or three qualifying children with valid SSNs, list them on Schedule EIC in the same order as they are listed here. If the taxpayer's EIC was reduced or disallowed for a year after 1996, see Pub. 596 to see if **Form 8862** must be filed. Go to line 20.

Note. If there is more than one child, complete lines 8 through 14 for the other child(ren) (but for no more than three qualifying children).

73

Part III **Taxpayers Without a Qualifying Child**

16 Was the taxpayer's main home, and the main home of the taxpayer's spouse if filing jointly, in the United States for more than half the year? (Military personnel on extended active duty outside the United States are considered to be living in the United States during that duty period.) See the instructions below answering . . . . ☐ Yes ☐ No

   ▶ If you checked "No" on line 16, **stop**; the taxpayer **cannot** take the EIC. Otherwise, continue.

17 Was the taxpayer, or the taxpayer's spouse if filing jointly, at least age 25 but under age 65 at the end of 2015? See the instructions before answering . . . . ☐ Yes ☐ No

   ▶ If you checked "No" on line 17, **stop**; the taxpayer **cannot** take the EIC. Otherwise, continue.

18 Is the taxpayer eligible to be claimed as a dependent on anyone else's federal income tax return for 2015? If the taxpayer's filing status is married filing jointly, check "No". . . . . ☐ Yes ☐ No

   ▶ If you checked "Yes" on line 18, **stop**; the taxpayer **cannot** take the EIC. Otherwise, continue.

19 Are the taxpayer's **earned income** and **adjusted gross income** each less than the limit that applies to the taxpayer for 2015? See instructions . . . . ☐ Yes ☐ No

   ▶ If you checked "No" on line 19, **stop**; the taxpayer **cannot** take the EIC. If you checked "Yes" on line 19, the taxpayer can take the EIC. If the taxpayer's EIC was reduced or disallowed for a year after 1996, see Pub. 596 to find out if **Form 8862** must be filed. Go to line 20.

Part IV **Due Diligence Requirements**

20 Did you complete Form 8867 based on current information provided by the taxpayer or reasonably obtained by you? . . . . ☒ Yes ☐ No

21 Did you complete the EIC worksheet found in the Form 1040, 1040A, or 1040EZ instructions (or your own worksheet that provides the same information as the 1040, 1040A, or 1040EZ worksheet)? . . . . ☒ Yes ☐ No

22 If any qualifying child was not the taxpayer's son or daughter, do you know or did you ask why the parents were not claiming the child? . . . . ☐ Yes ☐ No ☒ Does not apply

23 If the answer to question 13a is "Yes" (indicating that the child lived for more than half the year with someone else who could claim the child for the EIC), did you explain the tiebreaker rules and possible consequences of another person claiming your client's qualifying child? . . . . ☒ Yes ☐ No Does not apply

24 Did you ask this taxpayer any additional questions that are necessary to meet your knowledge requirement? See the instructions before answering . . . . ☒ Yes ☐ No Does not apply

To comply with the EIC knowledge requirement, you must not know or have reason to know that any information used to determine the taxpayer's eligibility for, and the amount of, the EIC is incorrect. You may not ignore the implications of information furnished to you or known by you, and you must make reasonable inquiries if the information furnished to you appears to be incorrect, inconsistent, or incomplete. At the time you make these inquiries, you must document in your files the inquiries you made and the taxpayer's responses.

25 Did you document (a) the taxpayer's answer to question 22 (if applicable), (b) whether you explained the tiebreaker rules to the taxpayer and any additional information you got from the taxpayer as a result, and (c) any additional questions you asked and the taxpayer's answers? . . . . ☒ Yes ☐ No Does not apply

▶ You have complied with all the due diligence requirements if you:
1. Completed the actions described on lines 20 and 21 and checked "Yes" on those lines,
2. Completed the actions described on lines 22, 23, 24, and 25 (if they apply) and checked "Yes" (or "Does not apply") on those lines,
3. Submit Form 8867 in the manner required, **and**
4. Keep all five of the following records for 3 years from the latest of the dates specified in the instructions under Document Retention:

   a. Form 8867,
   b. The EIC worksheet(s) or your own worksheet(s),
   c. Copies of any taxpayer documents you relied on to determine eligibility for or amount of EIC,
   d. A record of how, when, and from whom the information used to prepare the form and worksheet(s) was obtained, and
   e. A record of any additional questions you asked and your client's answers.

▶ You have not complied with all the due diligence requirements if you checked "No" on line 20, 21, 22, 23, 24, or 25. You may have to pay a $505 penalty for each failure to comply.

Part V   Documents Provided to You

26 Identify below any document that the taxpayer provided to you and that you relied on to determine the taxpayer's EIC
    eligibility. Check all that apply. **Keep a copy of any documents you relied on.** See the instructions before answering.
    If there is no qualifying child, check box a. If there is no disabled child, check box o.

		Residency of Qualifying Child(ren)			
	a	No qualifying child		i	Place of worship statement
	b	School records or statement		j	Indian tribal official statement
	c	Landlord or property management statement		k	Employer statement
	d	Health care provider statement		l	Other (specify) ▼ _____
	e	Medical records			_____
	f	Child care provider records			_____
	g	Placement agency statement			
	h	Social service records or statement		m	Did not rely on any documents, but made notes in file
			X	n	Did not rely on any documents
		Disability of Qualifying Child(ren)			
X	o	No disabled child		s	Other (specify) ▼ _____
	p	Doctor statement			_____
	q	Other health care provider statement			_____
	r	Social services agency or program statement		t	Did not rely on any documents, but made notes in file
				u	Did not rely on any documents

27 If a Schedule C is included with this return, identify below the information that the taxpayer provided to you and that you relied
    on to prepare the Schedule C. Check all that apply. **Keep a copy of any documents you relied on.** See the instructions
    before answering. If there is no Schedule C, check box a.

		Documents or Other Information			
X	a	No Schedule C		h	Bank statements
	b	Business license		i	Reconstruction of income and expenses
	c	Forms 1099		j	Other (specify) ▼
	d	Records of gross receipts provided by taxpayer			
	e	Taxpayer summary of income			
	f	Records of expenses provided by taxpayer		k	Did not rely on any documents, but made notes in file
	g	Taxpayer summary of expenses		l	Did not rely on any documents

FDA   15 88674   BWF 1040   Form Software Copyright 1996 – 2016 HRB Tax Group, Inc.   Form **8867** (2015)

-75

Form 8879

Department of the Treasury
Internal Revenue Service

.S e-file Signature Authorizã n

▶ Do not send to the IRS. This is not a tax return.
▶ Keep this form for your records.
▶ Information about Form 8879 and its instructions is at www.irs.gov/form8879.

CLIENT COPY

2015

Submission Identification Number (SID) ▶

Taxpayer's name	Social security number
Spouse's name	Spouse's social security number

Part I · Tax Return Information — Tax Year Ending December 31, 2015 (Whole Dollars Only)

1 Adjusted gross income (Form 1040, line 38; Form 1040A, line 22; Form 1040EZ, line 4) ·	**1**	5,376
2 Total tax (Form 1040, line 63; Form 1040A, line 39; Form 1040EZ, line 12) ·	**2**	
3 Federal income tax withheld (Form 1040, line 64; Form 1040A, line 40; Form 1040EZ, line 7) · · · · · · · · · · · · · · ·	**3**	68
4 Refund (Form 1040, line 76a; Form 1040A, line 48a; Form 1040EZ, line 13a; Form 1040-SS, Part I, line 13a) · · · · ·	**4**	1,589
5 Amount you owe (Form 1040, line 78; Form 1040A, line 50; Form 1040EZ, line 14) ·	**5**	

Part II · Taxpayer Declaration and Signature Authorization (Be sure you get and keep a copy of your return)

Under penalties of perjury, I declare that I have examined a copy of my electronic individual income tax return and accompanying schedules and statements for the tax year ending December 31, 2015, and to the best of my knowledge and belief, it is true, correct, and complete. I further declare that the amounts in Part I above are the amounts from my electronic income tax return. I consent to allow my intermediate service provider, transmitter, or electronic return originator (ERO) to send my return to the IRS and to receive from the IRS **(a)** an acknowledgment of receipt or reason for rejection of the transmission, **(b)** the reason for any delay in processing the return or refund, and **(c)** the date of any refund. If applicable, I authorize the U.S. Treasury and its designated Financial Agent to initiate an ACH electronic funds withdrawal (direct debit) entry to the financial institution account indicated in the tax preparation software for payment of my federal taxes owed on this return and/or a payment of estimated tax, and the financial institution to debit the entry to this account. This authorization is to remain in full force and effect until I notify the U.S. Treasury Financial Agent to terminate the authorization. To revoke (cancel) a payment, I must contact the U.S. Treasury Financial Agent at 1-888-353-4537. Payment cancellation requests must be received no later than 2 business days prior to the payment (settlement) date. I also authorize the financial institutions involved in the processing of the electronic payment of taxes to receive confidential information necessary to answer inquiries and resolve issues related to the payment. I further acknowledge that the personal identification number (PIN) below is my signature for my electronic income tax return and, if applicable, my Electronic Funds Withdrawal Consent.

Taxpayer's PIN: check one box only

[X] I authorize **HRB TAX GROUP INC** to enter or generate my PIN | 11783
                     ERO firm name

as my signature on my tax year 2015 electronically filed income tax return.

Enter five digits, but do not enter all zeros

[ ] I will enter my PIN as my signature on my tax year 2015 electronically filed income tax return. Check this box only if you are entering your own PIN **and** your return is filed using the Practitioner PIN method. The ERO must complete Part III below.

Your signature ▶ **Signature and Date on file**   Date ▶ _____

Spouse's PIN: check one box only

[ ] I authorize _____ to enter or generate my PIN | _____
                     ERO firm name

as my signature on my tax year 2015 electronically filed income tax return.

Enter five digits, but do not enter all zeros

[ ] I will enter my PIN as my signature on my tax year 2015 electronically filed income tax return. Check this box only if you are entering your own PIN **and** your return is filed using the Practitioner PIN method. The ERO must complete Part III below.

Spouse's signature ▶ **Signature and Date on file**   Date ▶ _____

Practitioner PIN Method Returns Only --- continue below

Part III · Certification and Authentication — Practitioner PIN Method Only

ERO's EFIN/PIN. Enter your six-digit EFIN followed by your five-digit self-selected PIN. | 77178335624
                                                    Do not enter all zeros

I certify that the above numeric entry is my PIN, which is my signature for the tax year 2015 electronically filed income tax return for the taxpayer(s) indicated above. I confirm that I am submitting this return in accordance with the requirements of the Practitioner PIN method and **Publication 1345,** Handbook for Authorized IRS e-file Providers of Individual Income Tax Returns.

ERO's signature ▶ _____   Date ▶ 02-09-2016

ERO Must Retain This Form — See Instructions
Do Not Submit This Form to the IRS Unless Requested To Do So

For Paperwork Reduction Act Notice, see your tax return instructions.

Form **8879** (2015)

1S_8879CC

FDA   Form Software Copyright 1996 – 2016 HRB Tax Group, Inc.   C1111D

76

BWF
TAXABLE YEAR
2015   **California Resident Income Tax Return**

ATTACH FEDERAL RETURN

FORM
540

APE

15

A
R
RP

CA 93611   APT   161

01-26-1979

		Filing Status	
1	[X] Single.	4	[ ] Head of household (with qualifying person). See instructions.
2	[ ] Married/RDP filing jointly. See inst.	5	[ ] Qualifying widow(er) with dependent child. Enter year spouse/RDP died [ ]
3	[ ] Married/RDP filing separately. Enter spouse's/RDP's SSN or ITIN above and full name here		

If your California filing status is different from your federal filing status, check the box here . . . . ⦿ [ ]

6   If someone can claim you (or your spouse/RDP) as a dependent, check the box here. See inst . . . . . . ⦿ 6 [ ]

► For line 7, line 8, line 9, and line 10: Multiply the amount you enter in the box by the pre-printed dollar amount for that line.

Whole dollars only

7   **Personal:** If you checked box 1, 3, or 4 above, enter 1 in the box. If you checked
    box 2 or 5, enter 2, in the box. If you checked the box on line 6, see instructions ⦿ 7 [1] X $109 = ⦿ $ [109.]

8   **Blind:** If you (or your spouse/RDP) are visually impaired, enter 1;
    if both are visually impaired, enter 2 . . . . ⦿ 8 [ ] X $109 = ⦿ $ [   ]

9   **Senior:** If you (or your spouse/RDP) are 65 or older, enter 1;
    if both are 65 or older, enter 2 . . . . ⦿ 9 [ ] X $109 = ⦿ $ [   ]

10 **Dependents:** Do not include yourself or your spouse/RPD.

	Dependent 1	Dependent 2	Dependent 3
First name	⦿ [████]	⦿ [ ]	⦿ [ ]
Last name	⦿ [████]	⦿ [ ]	⦿ [ ]
SSN	⦿ [████]	⦿ [ ]	⦿ [ ]
Dependent's relationship to you	⦿ [DAUGHTER]	⦿ [ ]	⦿ [ ]

Total dependent exemptions . . . . ⦿ 10 [1] X $337 = ⦿ $ [337.]

11 Exemption amount: Add line 7 through line 10. Transfer this amount to line 32 . . . . ⦿ 11 $ [446.]

195   3101154

15 **CA2D1**   BWF 1040

92

Form 540 C1 2015 **Side 1**
Form Software Copyright 1996 – 2016 H RB Tax Group, Inc.

77

Your name: [REDACTED]   Your SSN or ITIN: [REDACTED]

Taxable income

12 State wages from your Form(s) W–2, box 16 .... ⊙ 12 | 4,011.

13 Enter federal adjusted gross income from Form 1040, line 37; 1040A, line 21; or 1040EZ, line 4 ..... ⊙ 13 | 5,376.

14 California adjustments -- subtractions. Enter the amount from Schedule CA (540), line 37, column B .⊙ 14 | 1,365.

15 Subtract line 14 from line 13. If less than zero, enter the result in parentheses. See instructions ...... 15 | 4,011.

16 California adjustments – additions. Enter the amount from Schedule CA (540), line 37, column C ....⊙ 16 |

17 California adjusted gross income. Combine line 15 and line 16 .... ⊙ 17 | 4,011.

18 Enter the larger of: Your California **itemized deductions** from Schedule CA (540), line 44; **OR**
   Your California **standard deduction** shown below for your filing status:
   ⊙ Single or Married/RDP filing separately $4,044
   ⊙ Married/RDP filing jointly, Head of household, or Qualifying widow(er) $8,088
   If Married/RDP filing separately or the box on line 6 is checked, STOP. See instructions ⊙ 18 | 4,044.

19 Subtract line 18 from line 17. This is your **taxable income**. If less than zero, enter -0- .... ⊙ 19 | 0.

Tax

31 Tax. Check the box if from: [X] Tax Table [ ] Tax Rate Schedule
   ⊙ [ ] FTB 3800 ⊙ [ ] FTB 3803 .... ⊙ 31 |

32 Exemption credits. Enter the amount from line 11. If your federal AGI more than $178,706, see instructions .... ⊙ 32 | 446.

33 Subtract line 32 from line 31. If less than zero, enter -0- .... ⊙ 33 |

34 Tax. See instructions. Check the box if from: ⊙ [ ] Schedule G-1 ⊙ [ ] FTB 5870A ⊙ 34 | 0.

35 Add line 33 and line 34 .... ⊙ 35 |

Special Credits

40 Nonrefundable Child and Dependent Care Expenses Credit. See instructions .... ⊙ 40 |

43 Enter credit name [ ] code ⊙ [ ] and amount ...... ⊙ 43 |

44 Enter credit name [ ] code ⊙ [ ] and amount ...... ⊙ 44 |

45 To claim more than two credits, see instructions. Attach Schedule P (540) .... ⊙ 45 |

46 Nonrefundable renter's credit. See instructions .... ⊙ 46 |

47 Add line 40 through line 46. These are your total credits .... ⊙ 47 |

48 Subtract line 47 from line 35. If less than zero, enter -0- .... ⊙ 48 |

Other Taxes

61 Alternative minimum tax. Attach Schedule P (540) .... ⊙ 61 |

62 Mental Health Services Tax. See instructions .... ⊙ 62 |

63 Other taxes and credit recapture. See instructions .... ⊙ 63 |

64 Add line 48, line 61, line 62, and line 63. This is your total tax .... ⊙ 64 |

Your name: ▮▮▮▮▮▮▮▮▮▮ Your SSN or ITIN: ▮▮▮▮▮▮▮

Payments

71 California income tax withheld. See instructions .... ⊛ 71 [   ]

72 2015 CA estimated tax and other payments. See instructions .... ⊛ 72 [   ]

73 Withholding (Form 592-B and/or 593). See instructions .... ⊛ 73 [   ]

74 Excess SDI (or VPDI) withheld. See instructions .... ⊛ 74 [   ]

75 Earned Income Tax Credit (EITC) .... ⊛ 75 [1,163.]

76 Add lines 71 through 75. These are your total payments. See instructions .... ◉ 76 [1,163.]

Use Tax

91 Use Tax. **This is not a total line.** See instructions .... ⊛ [   ]

Overpaid Tax/Tax Due

92 Payments balance. If line 76 is more than line 91, subtract line 91 from line 76 .... ○ 92 [1,163.]

93 **Use Tax balance.** If line 91 is more than line 76, subtract line 76 from line 91 .... ○ 93 [   ]

94 Overpaid tax. If line 92 is more than line 64, subtract line 64 from line 92 .... ◉ 94 [1,163.]

95 Amount of line 94 you want applied to your 2016 estimated tax .... ● 95 [   ]

96 Overpaid tax available this year. Subtract line 95 from line 94 .... ● 96 [1,163.]

97 Tax due. If line 92 is less than line 64, subtract line 92 from line 64 .... ◉ 97 [   ]

79

Your name: [REDACTED]   Your SSN or ITIN: [REDACTED]

	Code	Amount
California Seniors Special Fund. See instructions	● 400	
Alzheimer's Disease/Related Disorders Fund	● 401	
Rare and Endangered Species Preservation Program	● 403	
California Breast Cancer Research Fund	● 405	
California Firefighters' Memorial Fund	● 406	
Emergency Food for Families Fund	● 407	
California Peace Officer Memorial Foundation Fund	● 408	
California Sea Otter Fund	● 410	
California Cancer Research Fund	● 413	
Child Victims of Human Trafficking Fund	● 419	
School Supplies for Homeless Children Fund	● 422	
State Parks Protection Fund/Parks Pass Purchase	● 423	
Protect Our Coast and Oceans Fund	● 424	
Keep Arts in Schools Fund	● 425	
California Senior Legislature Fund	● 427	
Habitat for Humanity Fund	● 428	
California Sexual Violence Victim Services Fund	● 429	
State Children's Trust Fund for the Prevention of Child Abuse	● 430	
Prevention of Animal Homelessness & Cruelty Fund	● 431	
110 Add code 400 through code 429. This is your total contribution	● 110	0.

NOT AVAILABLE YET
DO NOT PAPER FILE
CLIENT COPY

Contributions

Your name: [REDACTED]   Your SSN or ITIN: [REDACTED]

Amount You Owe

111   **AMOUNT YOU OWE.** If you do not have an amount on line 96, add line 93, line 97, and line 110. See instructions. **Do not send cash.**

      Mail to: **FRANCHISE TAX BOARD**
           PO BOX 942867
           SACRAMENTO CA 94267-0001 .... ● 111 [   ]

      Pay online -- Go to **ftb.ca.gov** for more information.

Interest and Penalties

112   Interest, late return penalties, and late payment penalties .... 112 [   ]

113   Underpayment of estimated tax. Check the box: ● ☐ **FTB 5805 attached** ● ☐ **FTB 5805F attached** ·· ● 113 [   ]

114   Total amount due. See instructions. Enclose, but **do not** staple, any payment .... 114 [   ]

Refund and Direct Deposit

115   **REFUND OR NO AMOUNT DUE.** Subtract the sum of line 110, line 112 and line 113 from line 96. See instructions.

      Mail to: **FRANCHISE TAX BOARD**
           PO BOX 942840
           SACRAMENTO CA 94240-0001 .... ● 115 [1,163.]

Fill in the information to authorize direct deposit of your refund into one or two accounts. **Do not** attach a voided check or a deposit slip. See instructions.

Have you verified the routing and account numbers? Use whole dollars only.

All or the following amount of my refund (line 115) is authorized for direct deposit into the account shown below.

● Routing number [   ]   ●Type ☐ Checking   ● Account number [   ]   ● 116 Direct deposit amount [   ]
                               ☐ Savings

The remaining amount of my refund (line 115) is authorized for direct deposit into the account shown below.

●Routing number [   ]   ●Type ☐ Checking   ● Account number [   ]   ● 117 Direct deposit amount [   ]
                              ☐ Savings

IMPORTANT: See the instructions to find out if you should attach a copy of your complete federal tax return.

To learn about your privacy rights, how we may use your information, and the consequences for not providing the requested information, go to **ftb.ca.gov** and search for **privacy notice.** To request this notice by mail, call 800.852.5711. Under penalties of perjury, I declare that I have examined this tax return, including accompanying schedules and statements, and to the best of my knowledge and belief, it is true, correct, and complete.

Your signature
X   Date   Spouse's/RDP's signature (if a joint tax return, both must sign)
                                 X

Sign Here

It is unlawful to forge a spouse's/RDP's signature.

Joint tax return? (See instructions)

Your email address (optional). Enter only one email address. [REDACTED]   Daytime phone number (optional) [REDACTED]

Paid preparer's signature (declaration of preparer is based on all information of which preparer has any knowledge)
[   ]

Firm's name (or yours, if self-employed)   ●PTIN
HRB TAX GROUP INC   P01277350

Firm's address 1610 HERNDON AVE   ●FEIN
CLOVIS CA 93611   431871840

Do you want to allow another person to discuss this tax return with us? See instructions .... ● ☒ Yes   ☐ No

Print Third Party Designee's Name   Telephone Number
RENUKA JAYAKRISHNAN   559-324-8491

BWF
TAXABLE YEAR
2015
California Adjustments — Residents

SCHEDULE
CA (540)

Important: Attach this schedule behind Form 540, Side 5 as a supporting California schedule.

Name(s) as shown on tax return

SSN or ITIN
607-22-1783

Part I   Income Adjustment Schedule
Section A – Income

		A Federal Amounts (taxable amounts from your federal tax return)	B Subtractions See instructions	C Additions See instructions
7	Wages, salaries, tips, etc. See instructions before making an entry in column B or C 7	4011.		●
8	Taxable interest (b) _____ 8(a)			
9	Ordinary dividends. See instructions. (b) _____ 9(a)			
10	Taxable refunds, credits, offsets of state and local income taxes 10			
11	Alimony received 11			
12	Business income or (loss) 12			
13	Capital gain or (loss). See instructions 13			
14	Other gains or (losses) 14			
15	IRA distributions. See instructions. (a) _____ 15(b)			
16	Pensions and annuities. See instructions. (a) _____ 16(b)			
17	Rental real estate, royalties, partnerships, S corporations, trusts, etc 17			
18	Farm income or (loss) 18			
19	Unemployment compensation 19	1365.	1365.	
20	Social security benefits (a) ● _____ 20(b)			
21	Other income.			
	a California lottery winnings e NOL from FTB 3805D, 3805Z,		a	a
	b Disaster loss deduction from FTB 3805V 3806, 3807, or 3809 21		b	b
	c Federal NOL (Form 1040, line 21) f Other (describe)		c	c ●
	d NOL deduction from FTB 3805V ● _____			
				f ●
22	Total. Combine line 7 through line 21 in column A. Adding through line 21f in column B and column C. Go to Section B 22	5376.		13. ●

Section B – Adjustments to Income

23	Educator expenses .... 23 ●			●
24	Certain business expenses of reservists, performing artists, and fee-basis government officials........ 24			●
25	Health savings account deduction 25			
26	Moving expenses........ 26			
27	Deductible part of self-employment tax 27			
28	Self-employed SEP, SIMPLE, and qualified plans 28			
29	Self-employed health insurance deduction 29			
30	Penalty on early withdrawal of savings 30			
31a	Alimony paid. (b) Recipient's: SSN ● _____ Last name ● _____ ... 31a			●
32	IRA deduction 32			●
33	Student loan interest deduction 33			●
34	Tuition and fees .... 34 ●		●	
35	Domestic production activities deduction........ 35			
36	Add line 23 through line 31a and line 32 through line 35 in columns A, B, and C. See instructions .... 36 ●		●	●
37	Total. Subtract line 36 from line 22 in columns A, B, and C. See instructions........ 37 ●	5376.	● 1365.	●

UNLAYAO ▮▮▮▮▮▮

BWF CA Schedule CA.(540) (2015)

Part II Adjustments to Federal Itemized Deductions

38 Federal itemized deductions. Enter the amount from federal Schedule A (Form 1040), lines 4, 9, 15, 19, 20, 27,
and 28 .... ⓘ 38 [   ]

39 Enter total of federal Schedule A (Form 1040), line 5 (State Disability Insurance, and state and local income tax, or
General Sales Tax) and line 8 (foreign income taxes **only**). See instructions .... ⓘ 39 [   ]

40 Subtract line 39 from line 38 .... ⓘ 40 [   ]

41 Other adjustments including California lottery losses. See instructions. Specify [   ] ...... ⓘ 41 [   ]

42 Combine line 40 and line 41... ⓘ 42 [   ]

43 Is your federal AGI (Form 540, line 13) more than the amount shown below for your filing status?
   Single or married/RDP filing separately $178,706
   Head of household $268,063
   Married/RDP filing jointly or qualifying widow(er) $357,417
   No. Transfer the amount on line 42 to line 43.
   Yes. Complete the Itemized Deductions Worksheet in the instructions for Schedule CA (540), line 43 .... ⓘ 43 [   ]

44 Enter the larger of the amount on line 43 or your standard deduction listed below
   Single or married/RDP filing separately. See instructions $4,044
   Married/RDP filing jointly, head of household, or qualifying widow(er) $8,088
   Transfer the amount on line 44 to Form 540, line 18 .... ⓘ 44 [4044.]

NOT AVAILABLE YET
DO NOT PAPER FILE
CLIENT COPY

▮▮▮ ▮▮ ▮▮▮

Side 2 Schedule CA (540) 2015   195   7732154
15 CACA2 BWF 1040   ₽3

2015 CALIFORNIA DEPENDENT CONTINUATION

Dependent's Name	Birth Year	Dependent Social Security Number	Relationship to Taxpayer	Number of Months in Home
███████	2015	███████	DAUGHTER	12

NOT AVAILABLE YET
DO NOT PAPER FILE
CLIENT COPY

16_TCA1Q

DO NOT MAIL THIS FORM TO THE FTB

TAXABLE YEAR			FORM
2015	**California e-file Return Authorization for Individuals**		**8453**

Your first name and initial	Last name	Suffix	Your SSN or ITIN
▮	▮		▮

If joint return, spouse's/RDP's first name and initial	Last name	Suffix	Spouse's/RDP's SSN or ITIN

Street address (number and street) or PO Box	Apt. no./Ste. no.	PMB/Private mailbox	Daytime telephone number
▮	▮		▮

City		State	ZIP Code
▮		CA	93611

Foreign country name	Foreign province/state/country	Foreign postal code

Part I   Tax Return Information (whole dollars only)

1 California adjusted gross income. (Form 540, line 17; Form 540 2EZ, line 16; Long Form 540NR, line 32; or Short Form 540NR, line 32) **1**		4,011.
2 Refund or no amount due. (Form 540, line 115; Form 540 2EZ, line 32; Long Form 540NR, line 126; or Short Form 540NR, line 125) **2**		1,163.
3 Amount you owe. (Form 540, line 111; Form 540 2EZ, line 31; Long Form 540NR, line 121; or Short Form 540NR, line 121) **3**		0.

Part II   Settle Your Account Electronically for Taxable Year 2015 (Payment due 04/18/2016)

4		Direct deposit of refund	5		Electronic funds withdrawal	**5a** Amount		**5b** Withdrawal date (mm/dd/yyyy)

Part III   Make Estimated Tax Payments for Taxable Year 2016 These are NOT installment payments for the current amount you owe.

	First Payment Due 4/18/2016	Second Payment Due 6/15/2016	Third Payment Due 9/15/2016	Fourth Payment Due 1/17/2017
6 Amount				
7 Withdrawal date				

Part IV   Banking Information (Have you verified your banking information?)

8 Amount of ref. to be directly deposited to account below ~~NOT AVAILABLE YET~~ 13 The remaining amt. of my refund for direct deposit

9 Routing number _____ ~~DO NOT PAPER FILE~~ 13 Routing number _____

10 Account number _____ ~~CLIENT COPY~~ 14 Account number _____

11 Type of account:		Checking		Savings	15 Type of account:		Checking		Savings

Part V   Declaration of Taxpayer(s)

I authorize my account to be settled as designated in Part II. If I check Part II, Box 4, I declare that the direct deposit refund information in Part IV agrees with the authorization stated on my return. If I check Part II, Box 5, I authorize an electronic funds withdrawal for the amount listed on line 5a and any estimated payment amounts listed on line 6 from the account listed on lines 9, 10, and 11. If I have filed a joint return, this is an irrevocable appointment of the other spouse/RDP as an agent to receive the refund or authorize an electronic funds withdrawal.

Under penalties of perjury, I declare that the information I provided to my electronic return originator (ERO), transmitter, or intermediate service provider, including my name, address, and social security number (SSN) or individual taxpayer identification number (ITIN), and the amounts shown on the corresponding lines of my 2015 California income tax return. To the best of my knowledge and belief, my return is true, correct, and complete. If I am filing a balance due return, I understand that if the Franchise Tax Board (FTB) does not receive full and timely payment of my tax liability, I remain liable for the tax liability and all applicable interest and penalties. I authorize my return and accompanying schedules and statements be transmitted to the FTB by my ERO, transmitter, or intermediate service provider. **If the processing of my return or refund is delayed, I authorize the FTB to disclose to my ERO or intermediate service provider, the reason(s) for the delay or the date when the refund was sent.**

Sign Here	▶		▶	
	Your signature	Date	Spouse's/RDP's signature. If filing jointly, both must sign. It is unlawful to forge a spouse's/RDP's signature.	Date

Part VI   Declaration of Electronic Return Originator (ERO) and Paid Preparer. See instructions.

I declare that I have reviewed the above taxpayer's return and that the entries on form FTB 8453 are complete and correct to the best of my knowledge. (If I am only an intermediate service provider, I understand that I am not responsible for reviewing the taxpayer's return. I declare, however, that form FTB 8453 accurately reflects the data on the return.) I have obtained the taxpayer's signature on form FTB 8453 before transmitting this return to the FTB; I have provided the taxpayer with a copy of all forms and information that I will file with the FTB, and I have followed all other requirements described in FTB Pub. 1345, 2015 e-file Handbook for Authorized e-file Providers. I will keep form FTB 8453 on file for **four** years from the due date of the return or **four** years from the date the return is filed, whichever is later, and I will make a copy available to the FTB upon request. If I am also the paid preparer, under penalties of perjury, I declare that I have examined the above taxpayer's return and accompanying schedules and statements, and to the best of my knowledge and belief, they are true, correct, and complete. I make this declaration based on all information of which I have knowledge.

ERO Must Sign	ERO's signature ▶	Date 02-09-2016	Check if also paid preparer ☒	Check if self-employed ☐	ERO's PTIN P01277350
	Firm's name (or yours if self-employed) and address ▶	HRB TAX GROUP INC 1610 HERNDON AVE CLOVIS CA		FEIN 431871840	ZIP Code 93611

Under penalties of perjury, I declare that I have examined the above taxpayer's return and accompanying schedules and statements, and to the best of my knowledge and belief, they are true, correct, and complete. I make this declaration based on all information of which I have knowledge.

Paid Preparer Must Sign	Paid preparer's signature ▶	Date 02-09-2016	Check if self-employed ☐	Paid preparer's PTIN P01277350
	Firm's name (or yours if self-employed) and address ▶		FEIN	ZIP Code

For Privacy Notice, get FTB 1131 ENG/SP.

FTB 8453 2015

100

p5

TAB S
Witness List

WITNESS LIST

If necessary, the following individual(s) will provide testimony in support of Respondent's applications for relief from removal:

1.   Name: ████████████████████
Summary of Testimony: Respondent's mother will provide testimony regarding her relationship with Respondent, Respondent's struggles, rehabilitation and good moral character and the effect that Respondent's deportation would have on their entire family.
Alien Number: USC
Length of Testimony: 20 Minutes
Language: English

2.   Name: ██████████ - Sister
Summary of Testimony: Respondent's sister will provide testimony regarding her relationship with Respondent, Respondent's struggles, rehabilitation and good moral character and the effect that Respondent's deportation would have on their entire family.
Alien Number: USC
Length of Testimony: 20 Minutes
Language: English

3.   Name: ██████████ - Friend
Summary of Testimony: Respondent's friend will provide testimony regarding her friendship with Respondent and Respondent's good moral character.
Alien Number: USC
Length of Testimony: 10 Minutes
Language: English

TAB T
Criminal History Chart

CRIMINAL HISTORY CHART

Date & Docket No.	Conviction	Sentence
07/24/2007 F07904397	CPC § 484E(d) – Misd Credit/Debit Card Fraud	36 Months Probation 3 Days Jail
12/29/2008 F08902017	CHSC § 11377(a) – Felony Possession of Controlled Substance	24 Months Probation 2 Days Jail
12/29/2008 F08907500	CHSC § 11377(a) – Felony Possession of Controlled Substance	24 Months Probation 1 Day Jail

TAB U
Letter from Respondent's Sister

May 15,2016

████████████

Immigration Status: United States of America Natural Born Citizen

████████████

Hanford,CA. 93230

████████████

Relationship: Sister

Occupation: Dual-rate Supervisor, Table Games

Dear Immigration Judge,

    I am ████████████ the sister of ████████████. She has been a part of my life for as long as I could remember. She's the mother to my niece ████ who will be turning 1 on July 11th, 2016.

    Like any normal sibling relationship, we have had our ups and downs. My sister has always been a huge part in my decision making. She doesn't know it, nor do I ever tell her. ████████, is also my daughter Ava's godmother. I wish you could see how they are when they are around each other, you would think that they had their own language, laughing and giggling, it makes my heart melt. Aside from being an amazing sister, daughter, friend, her best role in life is being a mother to Mila. Ever since Mila was born, she became more motivated. She worked her fingers to the bone, just so she can provide for her daughter and give her a better life. At times it's hard for her and seems like she's reached her breaking point, but she pushes herself. Mila is her world.

    My sister has had her fair shares of unfortunate events, bad choices and I'm sure she has hit rock bottom a few times. But even after all the hardship and scrutiny she received from friends and family including myself, she managed to get her life back on track. She has a stable job, and completed a program for drug and alcohol abuse and became a certified counselor. She's got great relationships with her previous and current employers. She has been a caregiver for many years, a job that I personally feel is not for just anybody, it takes a lot of patience. And that's something my sister has a lot of. To her it's not just a job, she cares for her patients and their well-being. I know at times, it's tough for her, but her effort and dedication remains.

90

In life we are faced with obstacles, struggles, and difficult decisions. As humans we do make mistakes, mistakes that at times cannot be undone, or easily fixed. But we manage because that is our natural instinct. My sister is not perfect, neither am I, and neither are you, but that's ok because that's what makes us who we are individually. My sister Carissa, is a good and caring person. An amazing mother, daughter, and sister. She should be here in this country, with her family. The opportunities here are endless and she has got so much more to offer. And much much more memories to make with her daughter. I strongly recommend that she is not to be deported.

Sincerely;

Allyssa Unlayao

91

TAB V
Additional Letters of Support

To Whom It May Concern,

My name is █████████. I am a co-worker of ███████████████ at Alorica in Clovis, Ca. We handle customer service for a company that requires a strong work ethic and good character. ████████ has constantly shown her excellent work ethic and excellent character. She is responsible, a great teammate, and a true friend. I'm truly grateful to recommend her for any endeavor she pursues! I absolutely recommend her for US citizenship.

Stephen Guillen

US Citizen

93

To whom it may concern,

I am writing this letter in regards to ██████████ and her character as a person and employee. She has worked for me for three months now and has become a vital part of my team.

She is here every day and on time. She is such a generous person. She always assists her peers and just overall a very good person. She always places her needs behind everyone else's and is very hardworking and diligent employee. Having her at work is a great impact on our company. Her entire life seems to revolve around her job and being a good mother. I cannot say enough positive things in regards to how great of a person she is.

Thank you for your Time,

████████ _[signature]_

94

CERTIFICATE OF SERVICE

Re: ███████████████████████████

I, Christopher A. Reed, hereby certify that I am a resident of or employed in the County of Los Angeles, State of California over 18 years of age, not a party to the within action and that I am employed at and my business address is:

Law Offices of Brian D. Lerner, APC
3233 E. Broadway
Long Beach, CA 90803
Telephone: (562) 495-0554
Facsimile: (562) 608-8672

On December 13, 2016, I served a copy of the attached *MOTION TO CONTINUE* on the following person(s) by the following method(s):

Office of the Assistant Chief Counsel
Department of Homeland Security
606 S. Olive Street, 8th Floor
Los Angeles, CA 90014
(E-Service: LOS.OCC.E-Service@ICE.DHS.gov)

I declare under penalty of perjury that the foregoing is true and correct. Executed in Long Beach, California.

DATED: December 13, 2016

By:_____
Christopher A. Reed
Attorney at Law